THE BIG BOOK OF Beading Patterns

For **peyote** stitch, **right angle** weave, **square** stitch, **brick** stitch, **herringbone**, and **loomwork** designs

From the publisher of *Bead&Button* magazine

KALMBACH BOOKS

Kalmbach Books
21027 Crossroads Circle
Waukesha, Wisconsin 53186
www.Kalmbach.com/Books

Published in 2010
14 13 12 11 10   1 2 3 4 5

Manufactured in the United States of America

ISBN: 978-0-87116-424-7

The material in this book has appeared
previously in *Bead&Button* magazine or on
BeadandButton.com. *Bead&Button* is registered
as a trademark.

Publisher's Cataloging-in-Publication Data

The big book of beading patterns : for peyote
stitch, right angle weave, square
  stitch, brick stitch, herringbone, and loomwork
designs / from the publisher
  of Bead&Button magazine.

      p. : ill. (chiefly col.) ; cm.

  "The material in this book has appeared
previously in Bead&Button magazine or on
BeadandButton.com."
   ISBN: 978-0-87116-424-7

  1. Beadwork--Patterns. 2. Beadwork--
Handbooks, manuals, etc. 3. Jewelry making-
-Handbooks, manuals, etc. I. Title. II. Title:
Bead&Button magazine.

TT860 .B54 2010
745.582

Contents

Introduction

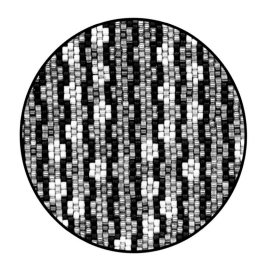

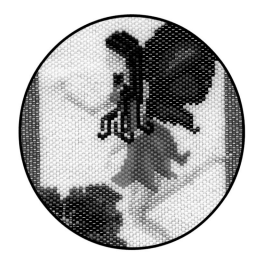

Say you have a favorite flower, or are fond of a particular Art Deco design, or have a weakness for fairies or pandas or lighthouses. By following a beading pattern like the 102 included in this book, you can create a beaded version of that image to wear or display in your home.

These patterns can be used in a variety of ways — a square or rectangular pattern can become the side of a purse or amulet bag, while other pieces can become the pendant for a necklace. Work loops at the top of the design, and you've got a wall hanging. Long, narrow designs make great bracelets, and small-scale patterns easily become earrings. We've even included patterns for a barrette, a business card holder, and a picture frame. Once you've practiced working with patterns, challenge yourself to create something as in-depth as the bonus projects, Jennifer Creasey's "Victorian spirit" necklace and Naomi Sakuma's "Loominosity" beaded lamp.

The patterns included here can be worked in a variety of stitches, including peyote, brick, square, and right-angle weave, or on a loom. The Basics section provides an explanation of how to work these stitches, as well as information about adding fringe to your beaded picture or creating a spiral stitch rope to turn your beadwork into a necklace. It's your work, so feel free to experiment and get creative!

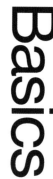

WORKING WITH THREAD

Conditioning thread
Use either microcrystalline wax or beeswax (not candle wax or paraffin) or Thread Heaven to condition nylon thread. Wax smooths the nylon fibers and adds tackiness that will stiffen your beadwork slightly. Thread Heaven adds a static charge that causes the thread to repel itself, so don't use it with doubled thread. Stretch the thread, then pull it through the conditioner.

Adding thread
To add a thread, sew into the beadwork several rows prior to the point where the last bead was added. Weave through the beadwork, following the thread path of the stitch. Tie a few half-hitch knots (see **Half-hitch knot**) between beads, and exit where the last stitch ended.

Ending thread
To end a thread, weave back into the beadwork, following the existing thread path and tying two or three half-hitch knots (see **Half-hitch knot**) between beads as you go. Change directions as you weave so the thread crosses itself. Sew through a few beads after the last knot, and trim the thread.

KNOTS

Half-hitch knot
Pass the needle under the thread between two beads. A loop will form as you pull the thread through. Cross back over the thread between the beads, sew through the loop, and pull gently to draw the knot into the beadwork.

Overhand knot
Make a loop with the thread. Pull the tail through the loop, and tighten.

Square knot
[1] Cross the left-hand end of the thread over the right, and bring it under and back up.
[2] Cross the end that is now on the right over the left, go through the loop, and pull both ends to tighten.

Surgeon's knot
[1] Cross the left-hand end of the thread over the right twice. Pull to tighten.
[2] Cross the end that is now on the right over the left, go through the loop, and tighten.

OFF-LOOM STITCHING

Flat brick stitch
[1] Begin with a ladder of beads (see **Ladder stitch**), and position the thread to exit the top of the last bead. The ends of each new row will be offset slightly from the previous row. To work in the typical method, which results in progressively decreasing rows, pick up two beads. Sew under the thread bridge between the second and third beads in the previous row from back to front. Sew up through the second bead added, down through the first bead, and back up through the second bead.
[2] For the row's remaining stitches, pick up one bead per stitch. Sew under the next

thread bridge in the previous row from back to front, and sew back up through the new bead. The last stitch in the row will be positioned above the last two beads in the row below, and the row will be one bead shorter than the previous row.

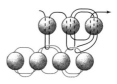

To increase at the end of the row, add a second stitch to the final thread bridge in the row.

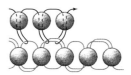

To increase within a row, add a second stitch to the same thread bridge as the previous stitch.

Tubular brick stitch
[1] Begin with a ladder of beads, and join the ends to form a ring (see **Ladder stitch**). Position the thread to exit the top of a bead.
[2] Following the instructions for flat brick stitch, pick up two beads to begin the row. Stitch around the ring in brick stitch.
[3] Join the first and last beads of the round by sewing down through the first bead and up through the last bead.

Crossweave technique
Crossweave is a beading technique in which you string beads on both ends of a thread or cord and then cross the ends through another bead.

Herringbone
[1] Start with an even number of beads stitched into a ladder (see **Ladder stitch**). Turn the ladder, if necessary, so your thread exits the end bead pointing up.

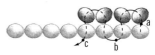

[2] Pick up two beads, and sew down through the next bead in the ladder (a–b). Sew up through the third bead in the ladder, pick up two beads, and sew down through the fourth bead (b–c). Repeat across the ladder.

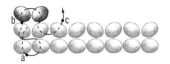

[3] To make a turn, sew down through the end bead in the previous row and back through the last bead of the pair you just added (a–b). Pick up two beads, sew down through the next bead in the previous row, and sew up through the following bead (b–c). Continue adding pairs of beads across the row. You may choose to hide the edge thread by picking up an accent or smaller bead before you sew back through the last bead of the pair you just added.

Ladder stitch
Traditional method

[1] Pick up two beads, sew through the first bead again, and then sew through the second bead (a–b).
[2] Add subsequent beads by picking up one bead, sewing through the previous bead, and then sewing through the new bead (b–c). Continue for the desired length.

This technique produces uneven tension along the ladder of beads because of the alternating pattern of a single thread bridge on one edge between two beads and a double thread bridge on the opposite edge between the same two beads. You can easily correct the uneven tension by zigzagging back through the beads in the opposite direction. This creates a double thread path along both edges of the ladder and aligns the beads right next to each other, but fills the bead holes with extra thread, which can cause a problem if you are using beads with small holes.

Alternative method

[1] Pick up all the beads you need to reach the length your pattern requires. Fold the last two beads so they are parallel, and sew through the second-to-last bead again in the same direction (a–b).

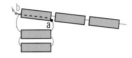

[2] Fold the next loose bead so it sits parallel to the previous bead in the ladder, and sew through the loose bead in the same direction (a–b). Continue sewing back through each bead until you exit the last bead of the ladder.

Peyote stitch
Flat even-count peyote

[1] Pick up an even number of beads (a–b). These beads will shift to form the first two rows as you stitch row 3.
[2] To begin row 3, pick up a bead, skip the last bead strung in the previous step, and sew through the next bead in the opposite direction (b–c). For each stitch, pick up a bead, skip a bead in the previous row, and sew through the next bead, exiting the first bead strung (c–d). The beads added in this row are higher than the previous rows and are referred to as "up-beads."
[3] For each stitch in subsequent rows, pick up a bead, and sew through the next up-bead in the previous row (d–e). To count peyote stitch rows, count the total number of beads along both straight edges.

Flat odd-count peyote
Odd-count peyote is the same as even-count peyote, except for the turn on odd-numbered rows, where the last bead of the row can't be attached in the usual way because there is no up-bead to sew through.

Work the traditional odd-row turn as follows:
[1] Begin as for flat even-count peyote, but pick up an odd number of beads. Work row 3 as in even-count, stopping before adding the last two beads.

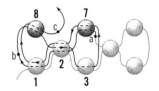

[2] Work a figure-8 turn at the end of row 3: Pick up the next-to-last bead (#7), and sew through #2, then #1 (a–b). Pick up the last bead of the row (#8), and sew through #2, #3, #7, #2, #1, and #8 (b–c).

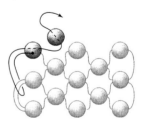

[3] You can work this turn at the end of each odd-numbered row, but this edge will be stiffer than the other. Instead, in subsequent odd-numbered rows, pick up the last bead of the row, then sew under the thread bridge immediately below. Sew back through the last bead added to begin the next row.

Tubular
Tubular peyote stitch follows the same stitching pattern as flat peyote, but

instead of sewing back and forth, you work in rounds.

[1] Start with an even number of beads in a ring.

[2] Sew through the first bead in the ring. Pick up a bead, skip a bead in the ring, and sew through the next bead. Repeat to complete the round.

[3] You need to step up to be in position for the next round. Sew through the first bead added in round 3 (a–b). Pick up a bead, and sew through the second bead in round 3 (b–c). Repeat to achieve the desired length.

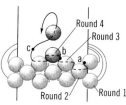

Two-drop peyote

Two-drop peyote follows the same stitching pattern as basic flat or tubular peyote, but you work with pairs of beads instead of single beads.

Start with an even number of beads divisible by four. Pick up two beads (stitch 1 of row 3), skip two beads, and sew through the next two beads. Repeat across the row or round.

Peyote decrease
[1] At the point of decrease, go through two beads in the previous row.

[2] In the next row, when you reach the two-bead space, pick up one bead.

Peyote increase
After finishing a row, pick up two beads and sew through both again. Snug them up to the beadwork, and then resume stitching in peyote.

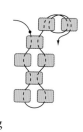

Zipping up or joining peyote
To join two sections of a flat peyote piece invisibly, match up the two pieces so the end rows fit together. "Zip up" the pieces by zigzagging through the up-beads on both ends.

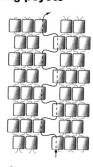

Right angle weave

[1] To start the first row of right angle weave, pick up four beads, and tie them into a ring. Sew through the first three beads again.

[2] Pick up three beads. Sew through the last bead of the previous ring (a–b), and continue through the first two beads picked up in this stitch (b–c).

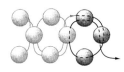

[3] Continue adding three beads per stitch until the first row is the desired length. You are sewing rings in a figure-8 pattern, alternating direction with each stitch.

Square stitch

[1] String the required number of beads for the first row. Then pick up the first bead of the second row. Sew through the last bead of the first row and the first bead of the second row again. The new bead sits on top of the bead in the previous row, and the holes are parallel.

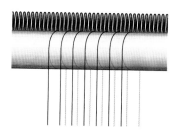

[2] Pick up the second bead of row 2, and sew through the next bead in row 1 and the new bead in row 2. Repeat this step for the entire row.

LOOMWORK

Set up the warp

Tie the end of the spool of thread to a screw or hook at the end of the loom. Bring the thread over one spring and across to the spring at the other end of the loom. Wrap the thread around the back of the rod behind the bottom spring and back to the spring at the top of the loom. Continue wrapping the thread between springs, keeping the threads a bead's width apart until you have one more warp thread than the number of beads in the width of the pattern. Keep the tension even, but not too tight. Secure the last warp thread to a hook or screw on the loom, then cut the thread from the spool.

Weave the pattern

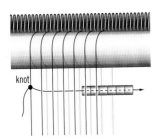

Tie the end of a 1-yd. (.9m) length of thread to the first warp thread just below the spring at the top of the loom. Bring the needle under the warp threads. String the first row of beads as shown on the pattern and slide them to the knot.

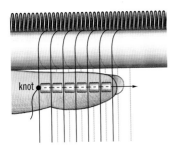

Push the beads up between the warp threads with your finger.

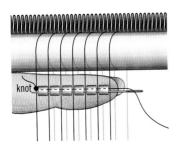

Sew back through the beads, keeping the needle above the warp threads. Repeat, following the pattern row by row. Once you complete the last row, secure the working thread by weaving it into the beadwork.

Decreasing

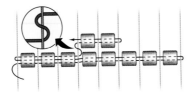

To decrease, sew under the end warp thread of the row you just completed, and sew back through the beads you'll omit in the decrease row. Wrap the working thread around the warp thread that will be the left edge of the decrease row. Pick up the beads needed for the decrease row, and position them. At the other end, skip the warps to the right of the beads that will be omitted, and sew back through the newly added beads.

Finishing the loomwork

[1] To remove the beadwork from the loom, carefully cut the warp threads as close to the screw or hook as possible.

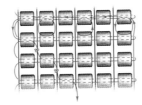

[2] Starting with the end warp on the right side, thread a needle, and sew through the first bead in the end row. Sew through the bead below it, the first bead again, and the next bead in the row. Repeat, moving down the end row. At the end of the row, sew into the beadwork, and end the thread.
[3] For the next warp, sew over and under the weft threads of the first two rows, then sew through a bead in row 2. Work as in step 2 to secure and end the thread. Repeat with the remaining warp threads, moving away from the end row as you end each thread.
[4] Repeat on the other end with the remaining warp threads, making sure to maintain even tension throughout the strip of loomwork. If you pull too hard, the beads will bunch up.

Whip stitch

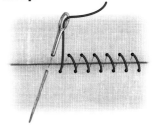

To join two layers of fabric with a finished edge, exit one layer. Cross over the edge diagonally, and stitch through both layers in the same direction about 1/16 in. (2mm) away from where your thread exited. Repeat for the length of the join.

Spiral rope

Bead chains made in spiral rope are good straps for amulet bags and purses or to display your wall hangings. Most spiral rope chains are made of two colors, one for the "core" beads and a different one for the "outer" beads.
[1] Condition 8 ft. (2.4m) of thread and use it doubled. String 4 core beads and 3 outer beads, leaving an 8-in. (20cm) tail.
[2] Go through the 4 core beads again in the same direction so the beads form a ring.
[3] Add 1 core bead and 3 outer beads. Skip the first core bead and go through the next 3 core beads.
[4] Go through the new core bead and adjust the new outer beads to sit against the first group of outer beads. Keep the tension firm as you work.
[5] Repeat step 3 and 4 until your rope is the desired length.

Fringing edges

Fringe is optional for amulet bags and beaded wall hangings, but if you're going to add it, don't skimp.

Thin, spread-out fringe often detracts from the beauty of a piece.

Basic fringes

When you make fringe, you need to snug up the fringe beads to the bottom of the beadwork so thread doesn't show between the two areas, but you don't want to tighten the fringe so much that it hangs stiffly with no movement or drape. In order to tighten fringe, it's absolutely critical that you do not split the original thread when you take your needle back up the fringe beads. It's easier to tighten a fringe if you hold the end bead or beads as you pull the thread.

Plain fringe

Come out a bead on the edge of the beadwork and string the desired fringe beads. Skip the last bead and go back up all the others. If you miss a bead as you are going back up the fringe, it will hang jaggedly and thread will show.

Picot fringe

[1] String like plain fringe, but skip the bottom three beads on the way back up.

Dangle bead fringe

[2] String the seed beads for the fringe and 1 to 3 more for a dangle loop. String the dangle bead and the same number of loop beads. Skip the first group of loop beads and go back up the fringe beads.

Loop fringe

String twice as many beads as needed for the fringe length. Don't go back up any of them. Instead sew through the next bead on the edge of the beadwork to form a loop.

Branched fringe

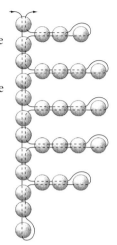

Branched fringe adds a lot of fullness. The branches can be as long as you wish. String at least 10 beads. Skip the last bead and go back up two to three beads. String two to four beads. Skip the last bead and go up the remaining one to three beads and two to three more beads on the main branch. Continue making short branches until you are back at the top of the main branch. If you wish, you can hang small accent beads at the tips of some of the branches.

Twisted fringe

After being worked for a while, thread has a natural tendency to twist back up on itself. You can use either parallel filament thread (such as Nymo) or twisted, plied thread (such as Silamide). With filament thread, you will have to add all the twist; with plied thread, you add more twist to what is already there. Twisted fringe is time consuming but the result is worth the trouble.

[1] Work with single thread and string twice the length of beads needed for a fringe plus a few more to allow for the shortening caused by the twist. Push the beads up to the beadwork.

[2] Grasp the thread a few inches below the strung beads and roll

it between the pads of your thumb and forefinger **(photo a)**. If you roll plied thread the wrong way, the plies will separate, so reverse direction.

[3] After each roll, grasp the thread with your other hand while you reposition your fingers for the next roll. You need to put a lot of twist in the thread for a good fringe—even more for long fringe or large beads. Keep your fringes consistent by counting the number of times you roll the thread.

[4] When you have rolled in enough twist, continue to hold the thread above the twist to keep it, but let the needle end dangle and run your free fingers toward the needle to relax this part of the thread.

[5] Weave the thread back into the beadwork for a few beads. To retain the

twist, hold the thread against the end bead until the last possible moment before pulling the thread tight through the beads **(photo b)**. If the fringe doesn't have sufficient twist, pull it out and twist some more.

[6] At this point, the twist has not been secured and will escape over time. You need to knot after each fringe with a half hitch around a thread in the beadwork to retain the twist. If you're making a continuous fringe, seal the last knot with clear nail polish by dabbing a drop on the knot with the tip of your needle.

[7] You may need to bend the fringe at the middle and shape it so the twist is even throughout the length **(photo c)**.

Picot edging

To finish the edges of a a flat band or panel, exit an edge bead. Pick up one to three beads to form your picot. Stitch down through the next edge bead, and up through the following edge bead. Repeat for the length of the beadwork.

Basics

We've included icons in each project that indicate what stitches are recommended for the design. These are often the stitches originally used or recommended by the pattern's designer, but in many cases, you may find that peyote and brick stitch are interchangeable, as are square stitch and loomwork.

Each pattern also features a color key that indicates the number of colors needed for the piece, and a suggested color palette. You can, of course, feel free to adapt the color selections to suit you.

You will find that some patterns include beads with dots or slashes through them. These symbols don't signify any special type of beads or unusual stitching — they are simply there to help differentiate between beads that are very similar in color, in order to make reading the patterns easier.

Many of the projects feature not only a pattern, but a photo of a stitched sample of the work as well. You may use these photos for ideas of color choices, variations, and finishing techniques, but don't feel that your piece needs to match the sample – feel free to be creative in your own color and finishing choices.

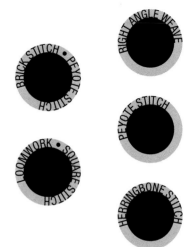

USING GRAPHED PATTERNS

Most patterns for bead stitches and loomwork are designed for size 11º Japanese cylinder beads. If there's no mention of another bead type, you can assume that the pattern calls for 11º cylinders. Cylinder beads are often referred to by their brand names: Delica beads by Miyuki, and Treasure and Aiko beads by Toho. With cylinder beads, use #10 or #12 beading needles and Nymo B (or an equivalent) thread. Condition the thread (see **Conditioning thread**) if desired.
[1] Start by sorting the required beads by color. Make individual piles on your work surface, or fill small, flat dishes with each color. Label each color with a number or letter to

match the color chart on your pattern, and arrange the beads in alphabetical order.
[2] If you're working with a peyote stitch pattern, the pattern rows are offset to match the position of the beads. A guide makes it easier to follow the pattern. To make a guide, lay a piece of paper over your pattern, and trace the vertical lines that separate the beads onto the paper's edge. Using a ruler, draw the first and last vertical lines about ¼ in. (6mm) long. Connect the lines along the bottom. Cut each vertical line to the ¼-in. mark. Fold over every other strip, and tape the strips down **(photo a)**. If you're working a large pattern, laminate your guide for durability.

To use the guide, place it over the pattern, and pick up the beads that show between the strips **(photo b)**. If you're following a pattern for herringbone, loomwork, or square stitch, the pattern rows form a grid. Simply place a ruler or sticky note along the horizontal grid lines to help you keep your place.
[3] Start at one corner of the pattern, and pick up beads for the first row. (Remember that in peyote stitch, you need to pick up the beads for rows 1 and 2. In brick stitch, you'll need to begin with a ladder row.) Work back and forth to stitch the subsequent rows, ending and adding thread as needed.

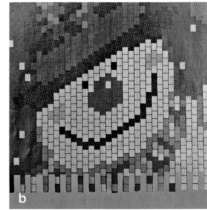

Animal
Patterns

Spider

The image of a spider has many ancient and interesting meanings. Spiders have a figure-8-shaped body and eight legs, and most have eight eyes; the lemniscate, the symbol of infinity, is also figure-8 shaped, making the spider a symbol of infinity.

Antonio A. Calles
Soledad, Calif.

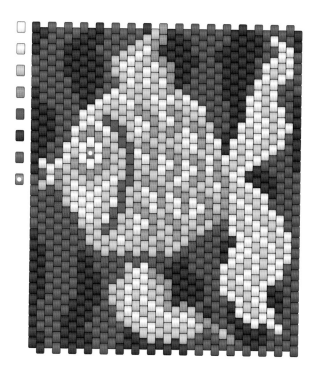

The idea of a tropical cruise really appealed to Cece as she trudged through a winter's snow, inspiring her to create this colorful fish.

Cece Meadows
Delafield, Wis.

Cockatoo

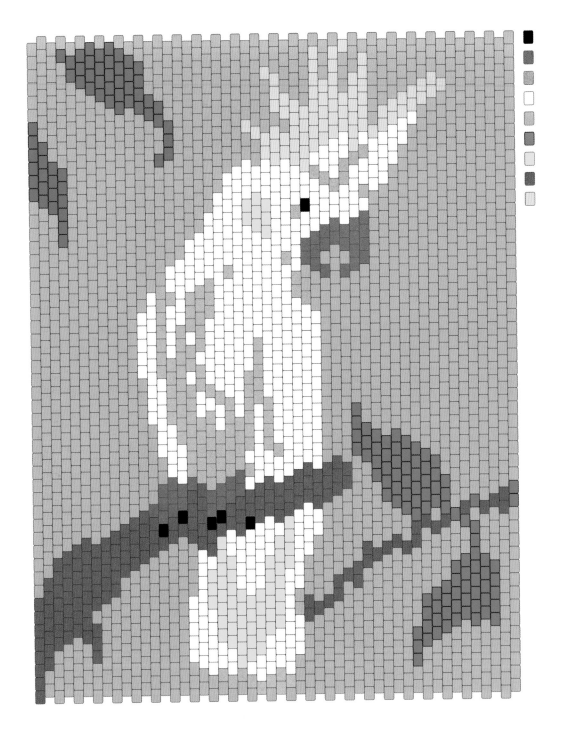

Polly want a cracker?

Bird lovers will delight in this charismatic cockatoo. Work in peyote stitch, and finish it as desired to make an amulet purse or wall hanging.

Melissa Johnson
Blanchard, Mich.

Ladybug

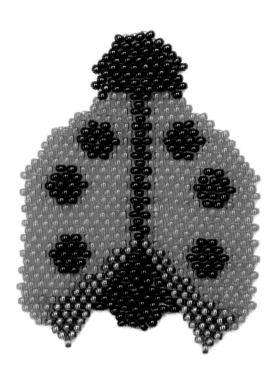

Cleopatra incorporated this pendant into a seed bead necklace embellished with glass leaves. The ladybug can be worked in brick or peyote stitch. When made with 8° seed beads, the piece measures $2^{3}/_{4}$ x $3^{1}/_{2}$ in. (7 x 8.9cm).

Cleopatra Kerckhof
Hemiksem, Belgium

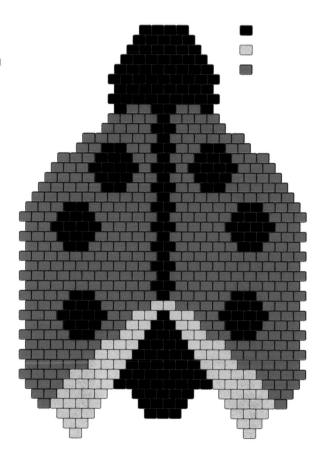

Butterfly bracelet

Butterflies spread their wings across a flat, odd-count peyote band. This dainty bracelet in spring colors is as light as a butterfly. Extend the pattern as necessary to fit your wrist. To taper the ends, decrease each row to form a point. Complete the bracelet with a spring-themed button and seed bead loop for the clasp.

Pamela Cottrell
Clinton, Ind.

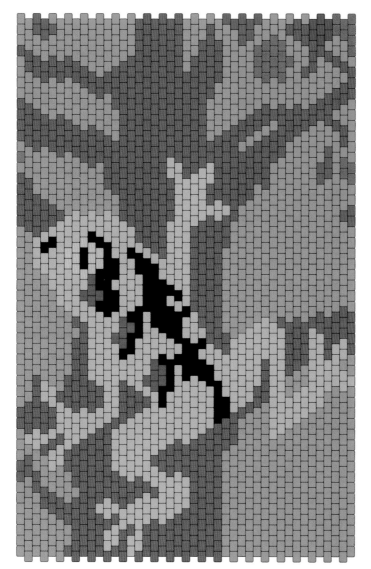

Stitch this peyote pattern in bright, tropical colors for an amulet bag straight from the rain forest.

Sharon Bateman
Rathdrum, Idaho

White horses

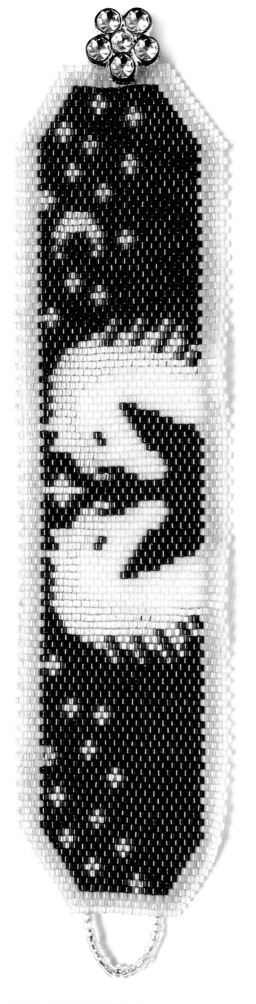

When Ronit saw a black-and-white image of a horse, she was captivated by its majesty and just had to design a pendant with the image it evoked: a white horse galloping through a moonlit field. She titled her work "Moonswept." The pendant measures 3⅜ x 2⅝ in. (8.6 x 6.7cm), and the bracelet measures 7 in. (18cm). Both are stitched in odd-count peyote stitch.

Ronit Florence
Toronto, Ontario, Canada

White horses

Butterfly wall hanging

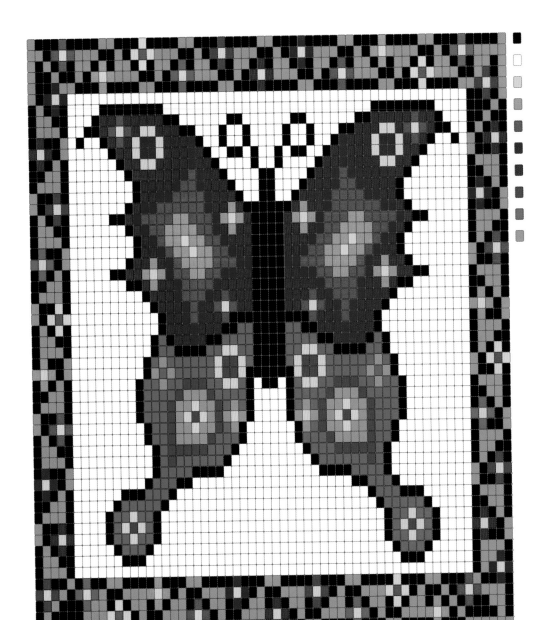

A floral motif in sunny summer shades graces this butterfly pattern. Designed for loomweaving or square stitching with 11º seed beads, this would make a beautiful wall hanging.

Danielle Easley
Albuquerque, N.M.

Bastet

If a cat could speak, Paulette believes her outlook on life could be summed up in one simple statement: "Thousands of years ago, cats were worshipped as gods. We have never forgotten." Bastet was the Egyptian goddess of cats. Show your love for cats by incorporating Bastet's image into an ornate amulet bag.

Paulette Biedenbender
Franklin, Wis.

Bluebirds of happiness

Take your own bluebird of happiness wherever you go. This cheerful little feathered friend hops across a bracelet that is worked in even-count peyote stitch and measures 6½ x 1½ in. (16.5 x 3.8cm).

Melody Marie Murray
Gresham, Ore.

Egyptian beetle

Isabee's son, who enjoys entomology, asked her to incorporate an insect into one of her designs. After seeing an Egyptian art exhibit in Chicago a few years ago, she was inspired to design this herringbone pattern of a beetle carrying the sun.

Isabee T. Demski
Reed City, Mich.

Scorpion

A larger-than-life scorpion stitched in square stitch or worked on a loom captures a Southwestern theme. Use size 11° seed beads in transparent turquoise and red, opaque black, and metallic silver. The completed piece measures approximately 4 x 7 in. (10 x 18cm).

Antonio A. Calles
Soledad, Calif.

Panda

Sharon's love for animals inspires many of her beaded pieces. This pattern for a wall hanging features a Giant Panda — the most recognizable animal in the world and one of the most endangered.

Sharon Bateman
Rathdrum, Idaho

Iguana

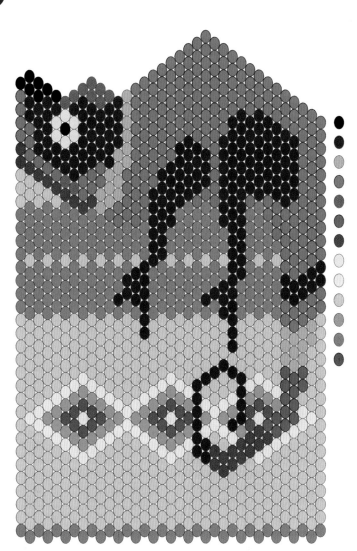

This iguana peyote pattern was designed just for fun. Make two panels and stitch them together for a great amulet bag, or use one as the centerpiece of a necklace.

Sharon Bateman
Rathdrum, Idaho

Hummingbird

The rich and vibrant color in this pattern gives it a tapestry-like appearance, so Jennifer made three tabs at the top to hang it from a decorative dowel. Work this pattern in peyote stitch. The finished piece is 3½ x 4½ in. (8.9 x 11.4cm).

Jennifer Creasey
Aleknagik, Alaska

Snake

Snakes always seem mysterious

and slightly amused. They present a playful temptation for nature lovers and all little boys! When designing this peyote stitch pattern, Sharon wanted to create a snake that would pop out from a collage of subtle greens. She envisioned a finished version with a surface and bottom edge embellished with fringe and leaf beads and the snake's head raised from the surface in a dimensional style.

Sharon Bateman
Rathdrum, Idaho

Dove

A white dove hovers above a red heart in this odd-count peyote stitch design. Create a bead picture by stitching an additional 10 to 12 rows at the top to wrap around a wire or wooden hanger. The design may also be adapted for a small bag.

Sharon Bateman
Rathdrum, Idaho

Gecko

This gecko pattern was intended for the front of a peyote stitch amulet purse. You can repeat it for the back, or just make a solid-colored back. Shannon was inspired by Southwestern gecko motifs and also by her own fondness for lizards, geckos, frogs, and fish.

Shannon T. Francis
Tahlequa, Okla.

Swans

Freda designed this necklace centerpiece for her best friend, Kim, who is a truck driver and thus seldom home to enjoy her collection of swans. Work the pattern in peyote or brick stitch, increasing and decreasing as needed. To make a panel for a wall hanging or amulet, stitch white beads to surround the swans.

Freda V. Smith
Ida Grove, Iowa

Dragonfly

Work this pattern on a loom or in square stitch. Amy prefers to use 15º seed beads for all her pieces so she can capture nature's details.

Amy M. Farnum
Saline, Mich.

Geometric and Abstract Patterns

PEYOTE STITCH • LOOM
STITCH • RIGHT ANGLE WEAVE
CH • LOOMWORK • SQUARE STITCH
RIGHT ANGLE WEAVE • BRICK STITCH • PEYOTE
WORK • SQUARE STITCH • HERRINGBONE STITCH
WEAVE • BRICK STITCH • PEYOTE STITCH • LOOM
ARE STITCH • RIGHT ANGLE WEAVE • HERRINGBONE S
HT ANGLE WEAVE • BRICK STITCH • PEYOTE STITCH •
ORK • SQUARE STITCH • HERRINGBONE STITCH • RIGHT
WEAVE • BRICK STITCH • PEYOTE STITCH • LOOMWOR
ARE STITCH • HERRINGBONE STITCH • RIGHT ANGLE
K STITCH • PEYOTE STITCH • LOOMWORK • SQUARE
RRINGBONE STITCH • RIGHT ANGLE WEAVE • BRICK
TE STITCH • LOOMWORK • SQUARE STITCH • LO
BONE STITCH • RIGHT ANGLE WEAVE • BRI
TCH • LOOMWORK • SQUARE STITCH •
WEAVE • BRICK STITCH • PEYO
STITCH • HERRINGB

Tamzara

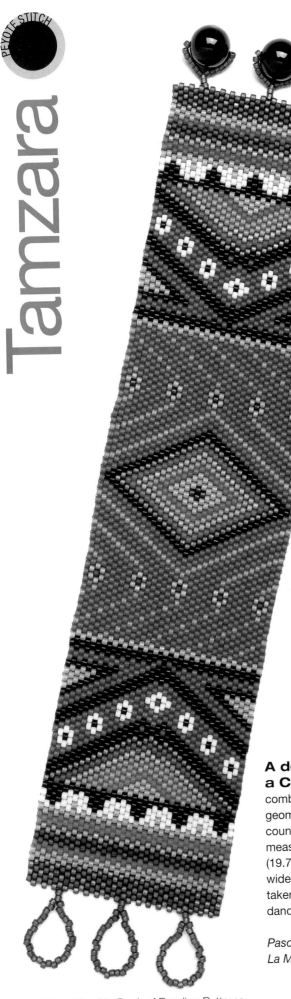

A design reminiscent of a Central Asian carpet

combines rich tapestry colors with geometric motifs. Stitched in flat odd-count peyote stitch, the beadwork measures approximately 7¾ x 1⅞ in. (19.7 x 4.8cm), which is perfect for a wide bracelet. The name *Tamzara* is taken from a traditional Armenian folk dance performed in a line or a circle.

Pascale Guichaoua-Mikovic
La Mulatière, France

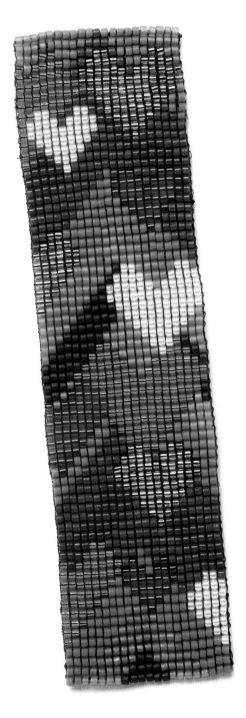

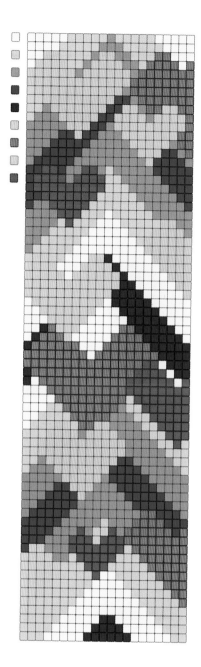

Hearts and more hearts

This pattern can be woven on a loom or worked in square stitch. The red hearts pop against a blue background. When stitched, the pattern is approximately 4¼ in. (10.8cm) long. To expand the pattern for a bracelet-length piece, you will need to add 21 rows of beads to each end of the design.

Mary Bedford
Portland, Ore.

Peyote pendants

Attach beaded dangles to these bold pendants with crimp end findings. Connect a bail to the top crimp end for stringing. For the symmetrical pendant, begin at the top, and work Panel A in flat, odd-count peyote. Work panels B and C in even-count peyote, decreasing as needed at the bottom. Connect panels B and C with cylinders draped between the inside edges. Attach a 1½-in. (3.8cm) crimp end at the top and a ½-in. (1.3cm) crimp end in the lower opening (file the edges down to fit the opening if needed). String beads on a head pin, make a loop, and attach it to the smaller crimp end. For the asymmetrical pendant, begin at the upper

Peyote pendants

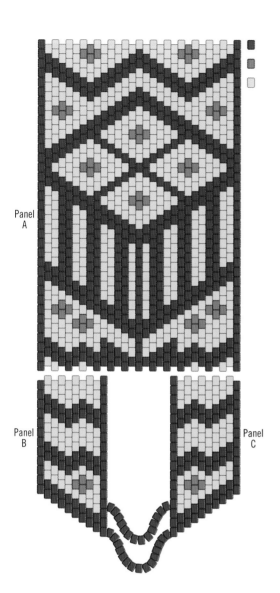

Panel
A

Panel
B

Panel
C

left-hand corner, and work the main panel in even-count peyote. Stitch the lower portion in odd-count peyote, decreasing as needed along the bottom. Use a 1½-in. (3.8cm) crimp end at the top, and a ½-in. (1.3cm) crimp end at the bottom. Attach a dangle as in the symmetrical pendant.

Mia Schulman
Gaithersburg, Md.

Art Deco inspiration

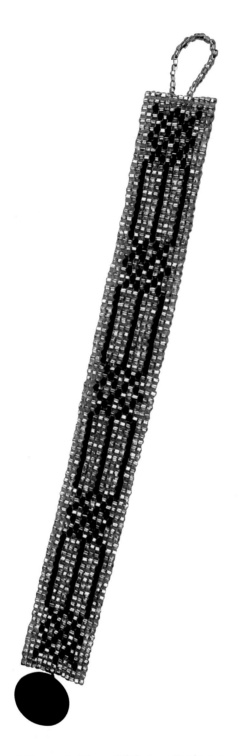

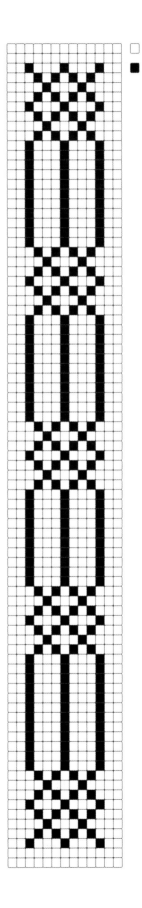

After visiting Eltham Palace, a restored 1930s Art Deco-style house in southeast London, Judith was inspired to recreate a classic Art Deco design. The square stitch bracelet measures 6¾ x ⅞ in. (17.1 x 2.2cm). The simple button-and-loop clasp maintains the clean lines of the design. The bracelet may be expanded or shortened by adding or removing a row of beads in each of the bar sections.

Judith Hind
Orpington, England

Victorian wave

After a day at the beach collecting shells and watching the waves, Pennie was inspired to make this bracelet. Work in flat even-count peyote stitch with 11º seed beads, decreasing at each end to create tapered points. Embellish each edge with 10º triangle beads. The finished bracelet measures 7¼ x ⅝ in. (18.4 x 1.6cm).

Pennie Espiritu
Clearwater, Fla.

PEYOTE STITCH

Karshi

The name Karshi comes from a city in Uzbekistan where gorgeous woven rugs are made. Inspired by these textiles, this pattern, designed in flat odd-count peyote stitch, makes a bracelet about 8 x 2¼ in. (20 x 5.7cm).

Pascale Guichaoua-Mikovic
La Mulatière, France

Starbursts

This bracelet uses 11° seed beads to create a 6-in. (15cm) band reminiscent of starbursts or snowflakes.

Danielle Easley
Albuquerque, N.M.

Frank Lloyd Wright motif

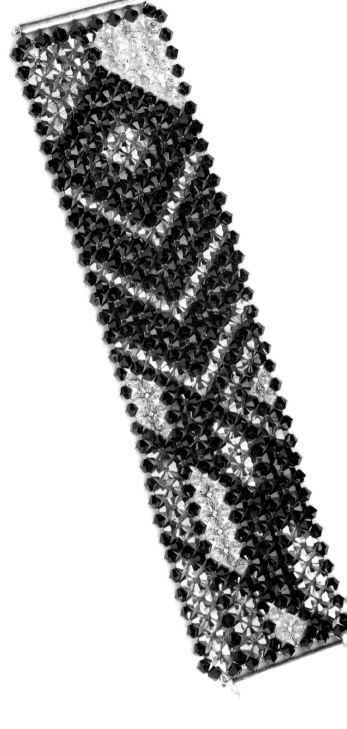

On a tour of Frank Lloyd Wright's home

and studio in Oak Park, Ill., Linda was fascinated by the play of light through his dramatic stained glass windows. She captured that luminescence and distinctive geometric patterning with dazzling Swarovski crystals. To make your own bracelet, work in right angle weave with 4mm crystals, starting with the rows outlined in red. The finished bracelet measures 7 x 1¾ in. (18 x 4.4cm).

Linda Landy
Miami, Fla.

Interlocking stars

Gloria took a new approach to a classic symbol by bisecting an interlocking star motif and stacking the halves for maximum impact. Your eye follows the movement of the pattern, allowing you to reassemble the star shapes. It can be worked in numerous colorways, from bright and fun to evening glam. This pattern is stitched in even-count peyote stitch to measure 6⅞ x 1 in. (17.5 x 2.5cm). Attach a three-strand slide clasp to wear it as a bracelet.

Gloria Simpson
London, England

Geometric pinwheel

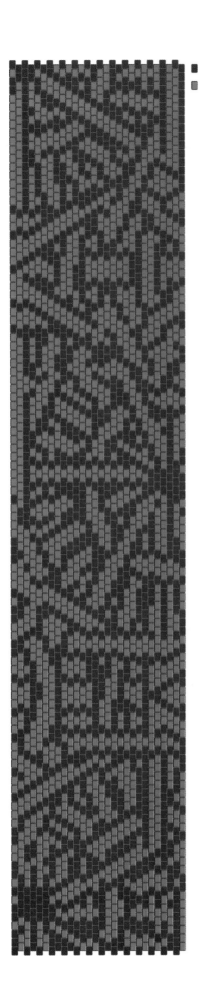

A playful way to give geometric patterns life and movement is to deconstruct them and piece them back together. Gloria used this technique to give a pinwheel motif a makeover, creating a dynamic pattern. Limiting the color palette to red and black gives the pattern even more punch. Worked in even-count flat peyote stitch, the bracelet is about 7¼ x 1½ in. (18.4 x 3.8cm).

Gloria Simpson
London, England

Hearts and diamonds

This ornate geometric design is a subtle square stitch heart pattern ideal for an amulet bag or cuff bracelet.

Elizabeth Liechti
Chicago, Ill.

Greek key design

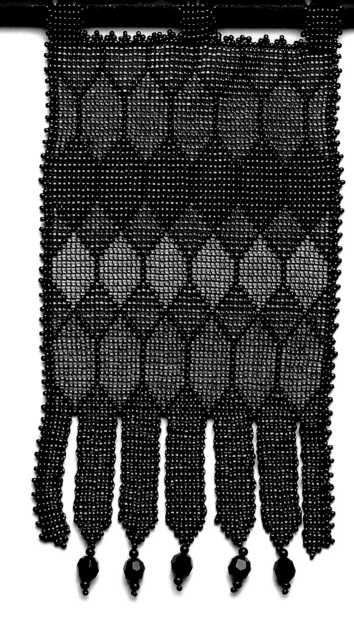

A traditional Greek key pattern

in dark blue and gold was a favorite motif during the 1930s Art Deco era. The bracelet is approximately 7 x ½ in. (18 x 1.3cm). Lengthen or shorten the band by adding or omitting a repeat of the main six-row pattern. Work a square stitch "button" for the clasp.

Judith Hind
Orpington, England

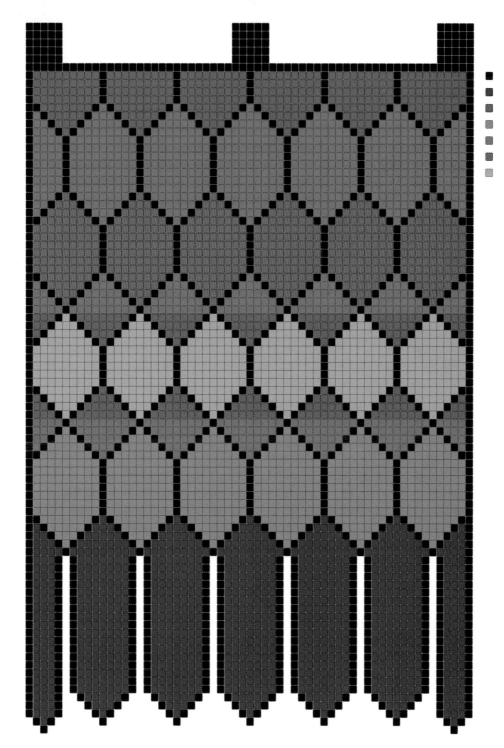

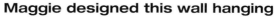

Stained glass

Maggie designed this wall hanging
to create the look of stained glass with a Victorian
mood. Finish the outside edges with a three-bead
picot and dangle a 4mm round bead, a 10mm
faceted round, a 4mm round, and an 11º seed bead
off the end of each of the middle five strips. Maggie
made the three hanging loops long enough to wrap
around a ⅜-in. (1cm) black dowel and secured them
to the back of the wall hanging.

Maggie Beese
Oshkosh, Wis.

Lovely and linear

Eileen enjoyed working up this simple odd-count peyote stitch bracelet so much that she's made it many times. Start at the top of the charted pattern and work down, continuing the pattern with no break in the black-bead branching. After stitching the bracelet to the desired length, end with three rows of beads, just as it started with the first three rows. Eileen embellished her edges with a three-bead picot of a 15°, a cylinders, and a 15°, and used 5/16-in. (8mm) buttons with beaded loops for the clasp.

Eileen Spitz
Boynton Beach, Fla.

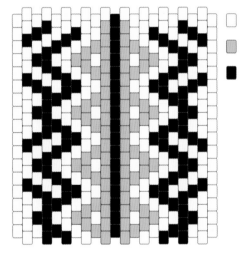

Colored blocks

Beginning at the lower left-hand corner, work in flat herringbone stitch to complete this abstract geometric cityscape.

Audrey Parramore
Tampa, Fla.

Alaskan tapestry

This tapestry took Jennifer 10 days to bead, averaging about seven brick stitch rows each day. The pattern could also be worked in peyote stitch. Jennifer likes to hang her tapestries on pieces of driftwood that she and her kids find.

Jennifer Creasy
Aleknagik, Alaska

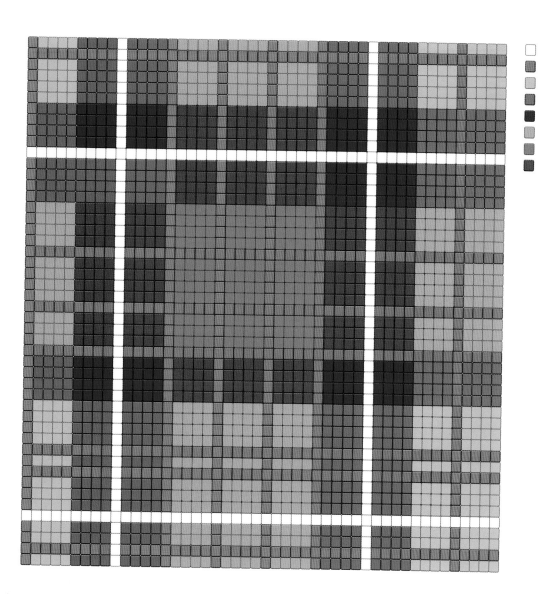

Dorion's family tartan, McDonnell of
Glengarry, was the inspiration for this pattern, which
she extended into a thick bracelet.

Dorion Cable
Southfield, Mich.

Neon diamonds

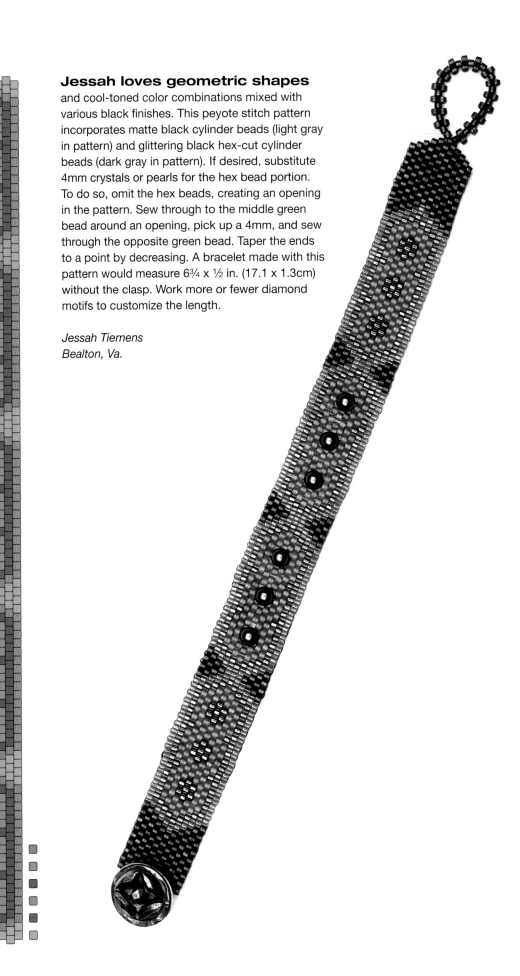

Jessah loves geometric shapes
and cool-toned color combinations mixed with various black finishes. This peyote stitch pattern incorporates matte black cylinder beads (light gray in pattern) and glittering black hex-cut cylinder beads (dark gray in pattern). If desired, substitute 4mm crystals or pearls for the hex bead portion. To do so, omit the hex beads, creating an opening in the pattern. Sew through to the middle green bead around an opening, pick up a 4mm, and sew through the opposite green bead. Taper the ends to a point by decreasing. A bracelet made with this pattern would measure 6¾ x ½ in. (17.1 x 1.3cm) without the clasp. Work more or fewer diamond motifs to customize the length.

Jessah Tiemens
Bealton, Va.

Celtic motifs

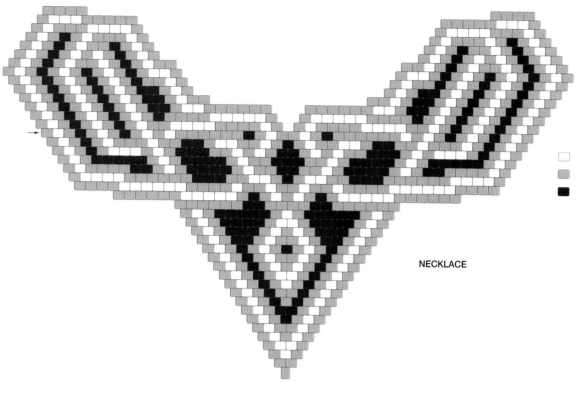

NECKLACE

EARRING

Lovely Celtic designs make for beautiful jewelry pieces. Start at the arrow and work the pattern for the necklace centerpiece in brick stitch. Make the earrings in peyote stitch and use smaller beads for the loops.

Bobbi Bongard
New York, N.Y.

Folk hearts

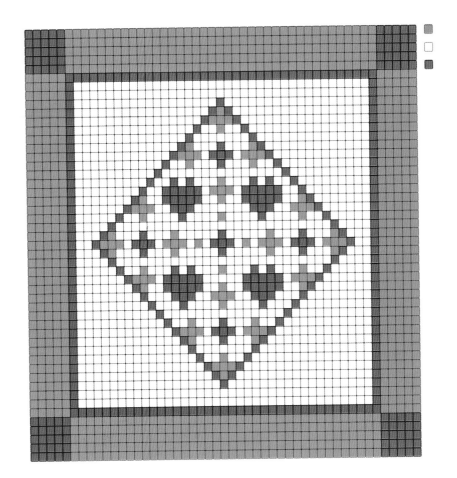

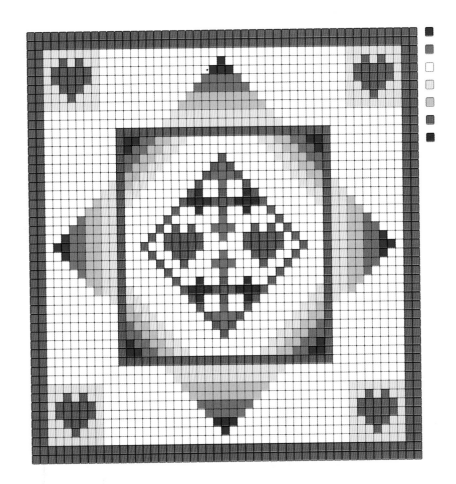

Folk hearts

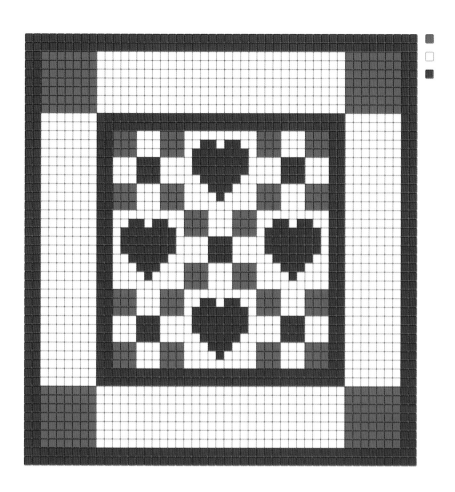

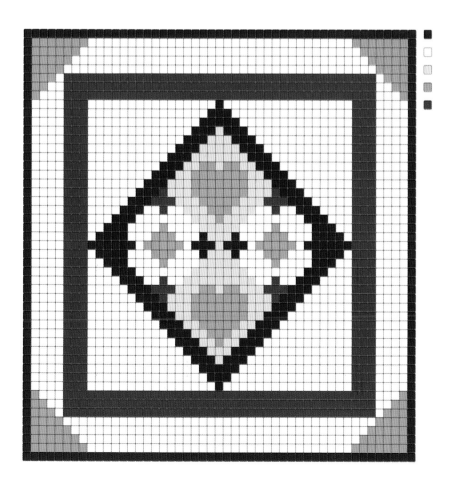

Laura's mother, Janet Price, designed a series of quilted wall hangings called *Folk Hearts.* As a gift to her, Lora re-created the patterns on her loom using Japanese cylinder beads. Naturally, her mother incorporated the beadwork into a new wall hanging!

Laura Price
Mississauga, Ontario

African mudcloth

Katherine's square stitch bracelet

designs were inspired by African mudcloth. She chose square stitch because she finds it more practical than a loom for small pieces. This stitch is also very sturdy, which makes it a good choice for jewelry that will get a lot of wear.

Katherine Richards

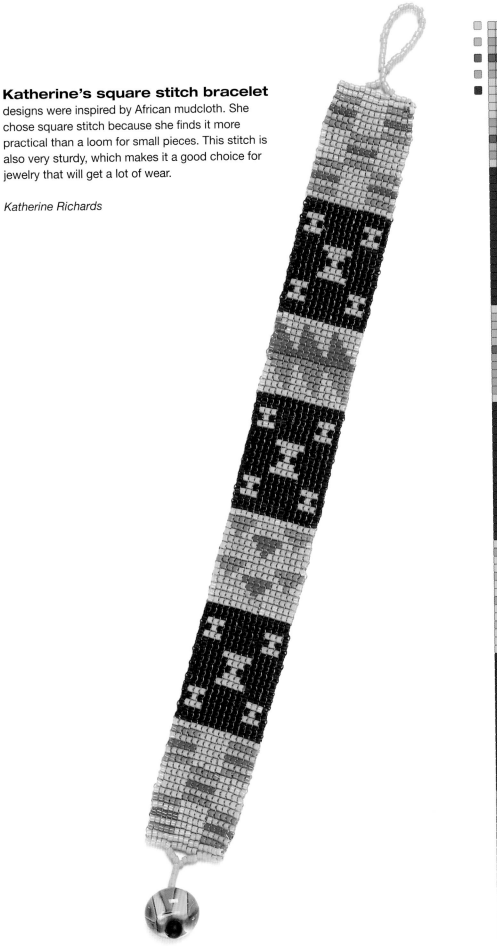

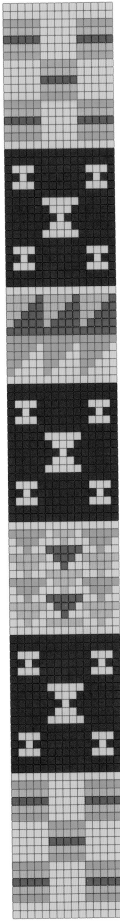

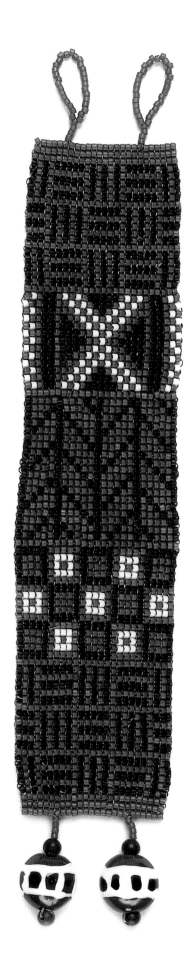

African mudcloth

SQUARE STITCH

African mudcloth

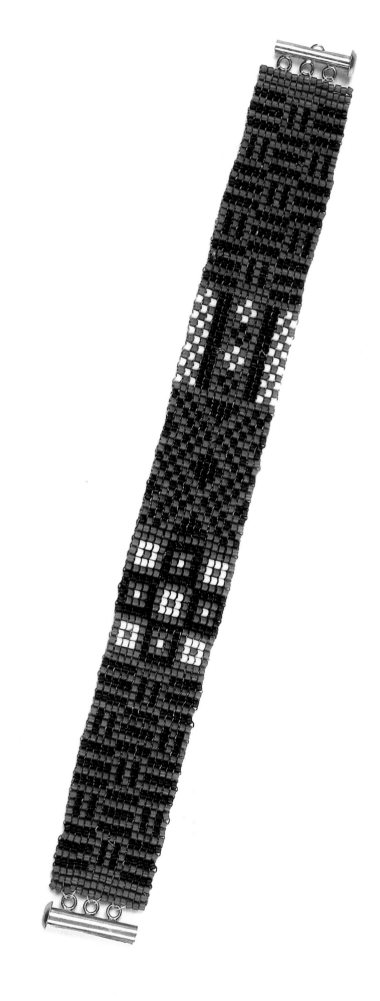

The circle contains repeated text: PEYOTE STITCH • LOOMWORK • RIGHT ANGLE WEAVE • BRICK STITCH • SQUARE STITCH • HERRINGBONE STITCH

Holiday Patterns

Kiss and tell

Lisa created this loomwork pattern of a kissing bride and groom for her cousin's wedding, but finds it equally appropriate for Valentine's Day.

Lisa Brideau
Middleton, Wis.

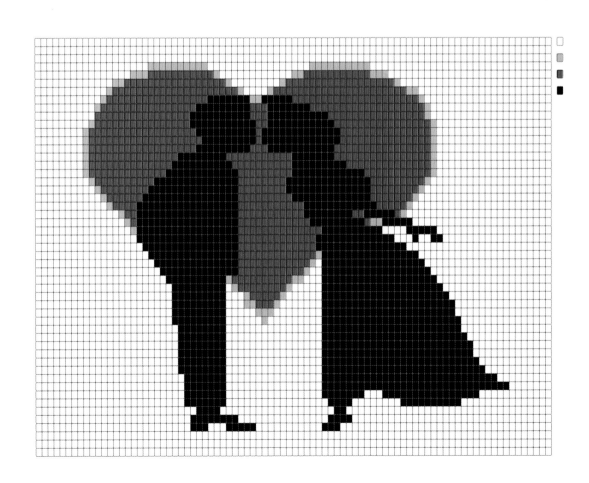

Bunny party

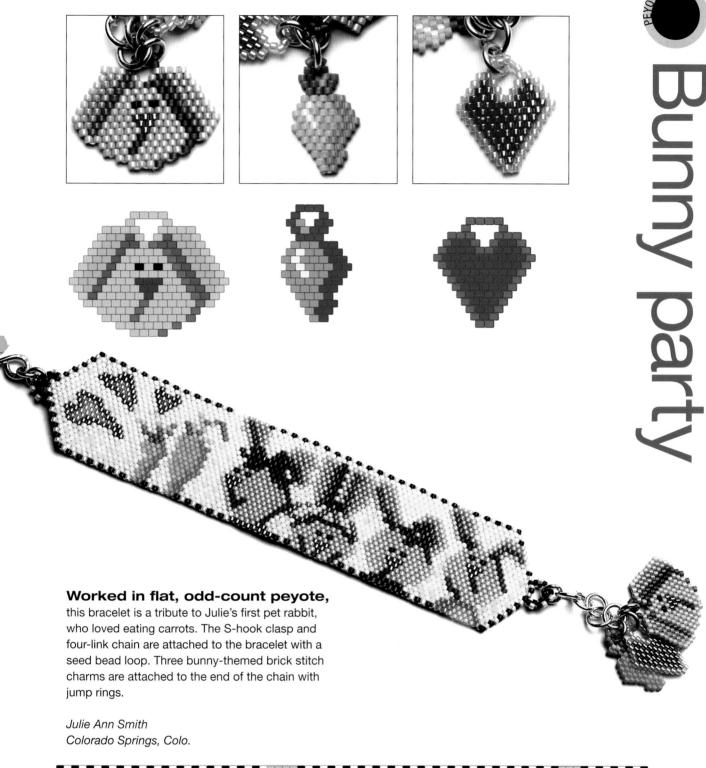

Worked in flat, odd-count peyote,

this bracelet is a tribute to Julie's first pet rabbit, who loved eating carrots. The S-hook clasp and four-link chain are attached to the bracelet with a seed bead loop. Three bunny-themed brick stitch charms are attached to the end of the chain with jump rings.

Julie Ann Smith
Colorado Springs, Colo.

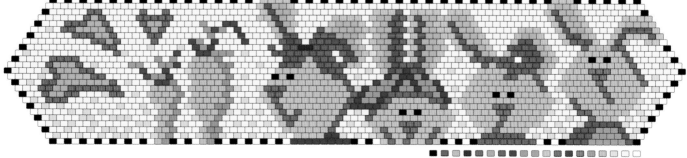

Wild hares

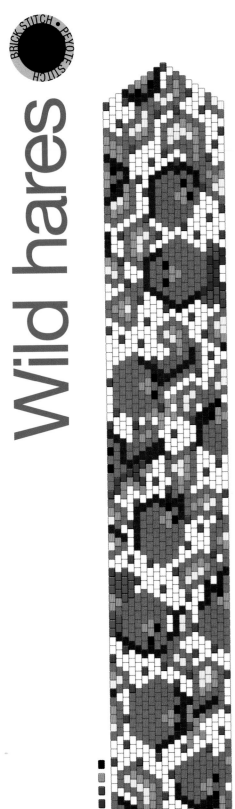

To make "Wild Hares," work in flat, odd-count peyote, beginning at one corner of the band. To taper the ends, follow the pattern and decrease each row to form a point. A seed bead loop and beaded toggle bar complete the bracelet. To make the toggle bar, stitch a strip of peyote that is 18 beads wide with eight beads on each straight edge. Zip up the ends to create a tube.

Julie Ann Smith
Colorado Springs, Colo.

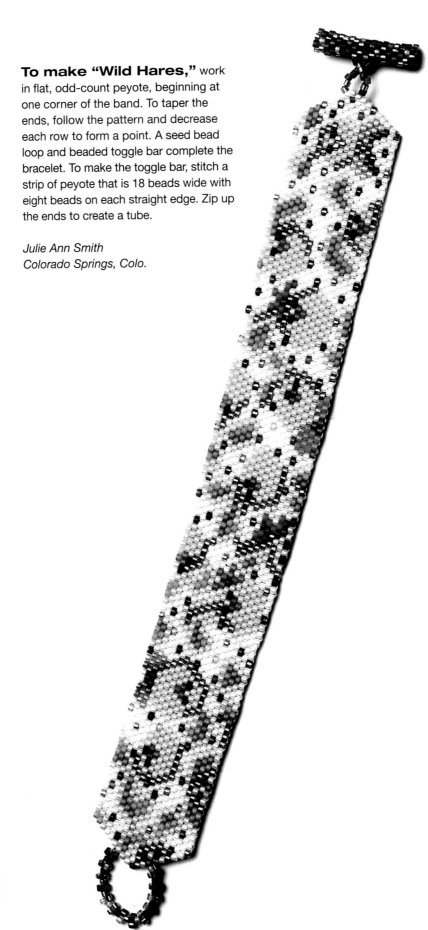

Star-spangled links

This festive 4th of July bracelet is constructed in two steps: First work the center band in flat, even-count peyote, then add the points with brick stitch.

Jennifer Creasey
Aleknagik, Alaska

Uncle Sam

Uncle Sam

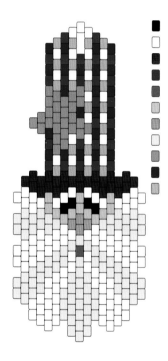

Show your patriotic spirit with Jennifer's Y-necklace pattern worked in brick stitch or peyote. The beard is made with opaque white 11º seed beads: Make the first loop as shown on the pattern, then increase the following loops by five beads each until you reach the center point of the pattern (middle red bead). The center loop will have 70 beads. Work the second side as the mirror image of the first. Adjust the pattern slightly for a matching bracelet. Pressed for time, but love the Uncle Sam theme? The fun earrings work up quickly.

Jennifer Creasey
Aleknagik, Alaska

American sweetheart

Use a palette of red, white, and blue to make this patriotic bracelet. You can change the pattern by switching to a red background with blue inverted hearts. If you work this pattern on a loom, here's one way to finish: After you cut the band off the loom, string bugle beads on groups of two or three warp threads at each end. String a crimp bead, a 6mm bead, and a clasp half over all 11 threads, and go back through the 6mms and crimp beads. Crimp the crimp beads, and trim the threads.

Donna Coverdale
Parkton, N.C.

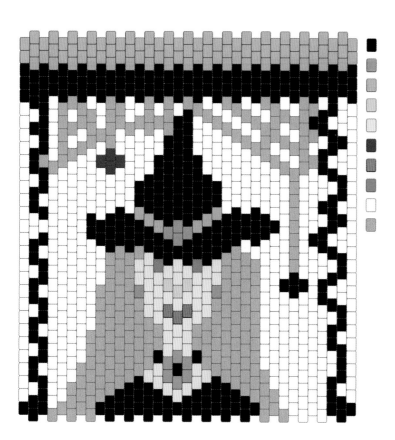

A good witch

Rhonda designed this peyote amulet for her mom in honor of her Halloween birthday, but is quick to point out that she's one of the good witches!

Rhonda Guy
Lexington, Ky.

Trick or treat

Make this two-sided design
in tubular, even-count peyote. Zip up the
side and add charms and fringe for a fun
Halloween accessory.

Jennifer Creasey
Aleknagik, Alaska

Mr. and Mrs. Bones

This creepy couple makes an adorable pair of earrings or bracelet charms. To make them without thread showing along the sides, work the patterns vertically in square stitch. Starting at the top of the center section, stitch two vertical rows, and continue stitching to add one side. Sew through the beadwork to the starting row, and stitch the other side. Make a small loop for hanging.

Rhonda M. Guy
Lexington, Ky.

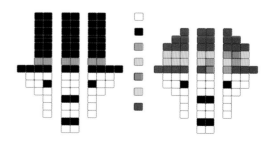

Snowman

After receiving an adorable snowman gift bag, Diane decided to adapt the image and graph it for a peyote pattern. For the wall hanging shown, she worked the pattern from the bottom up so the top portion of the pattern — the sky — could be extended until it was long enough to form a tube. The bottom fringe is a mix of white-lined and white cylinder beads and teardrops. Hang your finished piece from a wood dowel or make a wire hanger with 20-gauge wire.

Diane Schroer
Shelby Township, Mich.

Santas repeat

Carol has been designing patterns ever since a friend made a loom for her. This festive pattern is great for the holidays, and is easy to repeat to adjust the length of your bracelet. To create a buttonhole, work partial rows to create one side of the opening. Work a complete row to end the opening, then go back and work partial rows on the other side of the opening.

Carol Green
Toledo, Ohio

Rosy-cheeked Santa

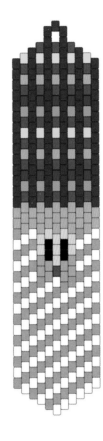

Add surface embellishments and cheerful colors to this peyote pattern to make your Santa come to life. Make a fun bracelet, and add matching earrings or a zipper pull.

Jennifer Creasey
Aleknagik, Alaska

Snowflakes

Celebrate winter with this charming bracelet. Work the band in flat odd-count peyote, then add a snowflake button, tapered ends, or a pretty picot edging to finish.

Sue Mertz

Holiday necklace

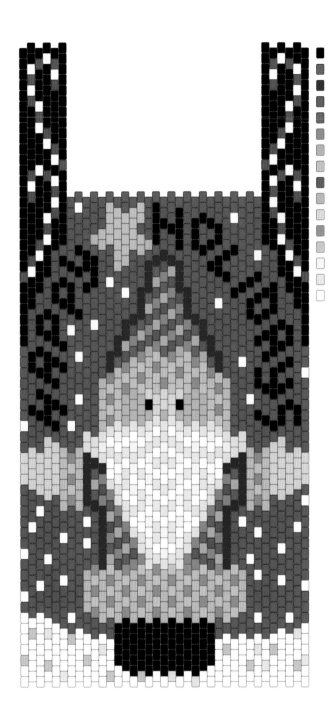

Add netted fringe and glass beads
to this vibrant holiday pattern for a one-of-a-kind
necklace that you'll love to wear or give as a gift.

Jennifer Creasey
Aleknagik, Alaska

Ornaments

Stitched in flat even-count peyote,

these holiday-color ornaments dance across a winter-white background. To finish each end, exit one of the two gold beads on the edge, pick up six gold beads, and sew back through all eight gold beads to form a loop. Use a small, gold-filled jump ring to attach half of a gold-filled clasp and a beaded loop. The bracelet band is 5⅝ x ⅝ in. (14.3 x 1.6cm).

Diana Hall
Roblin, Ontario

Santa and reindeer

PEYOTE STITCH

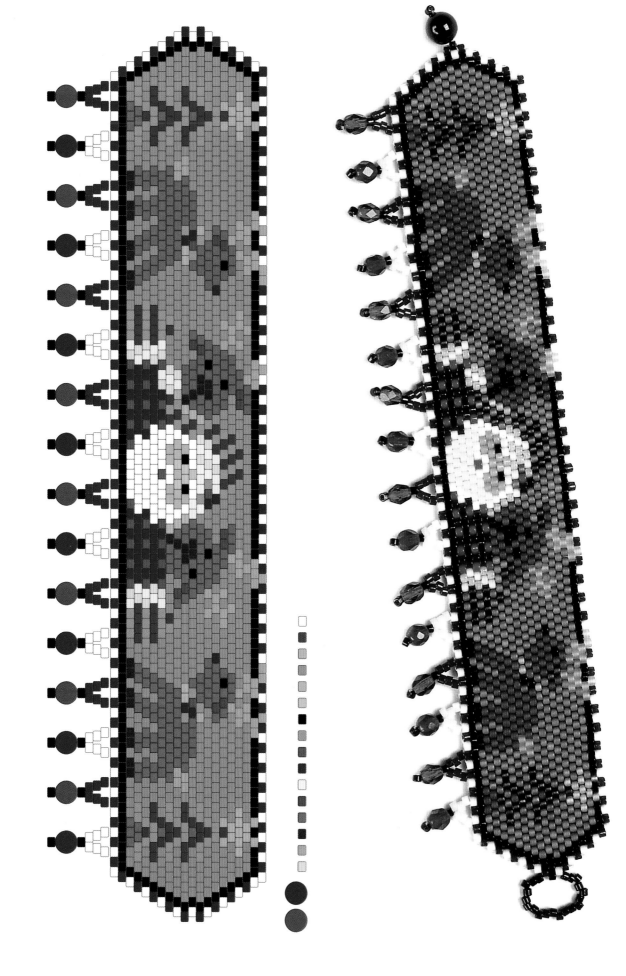

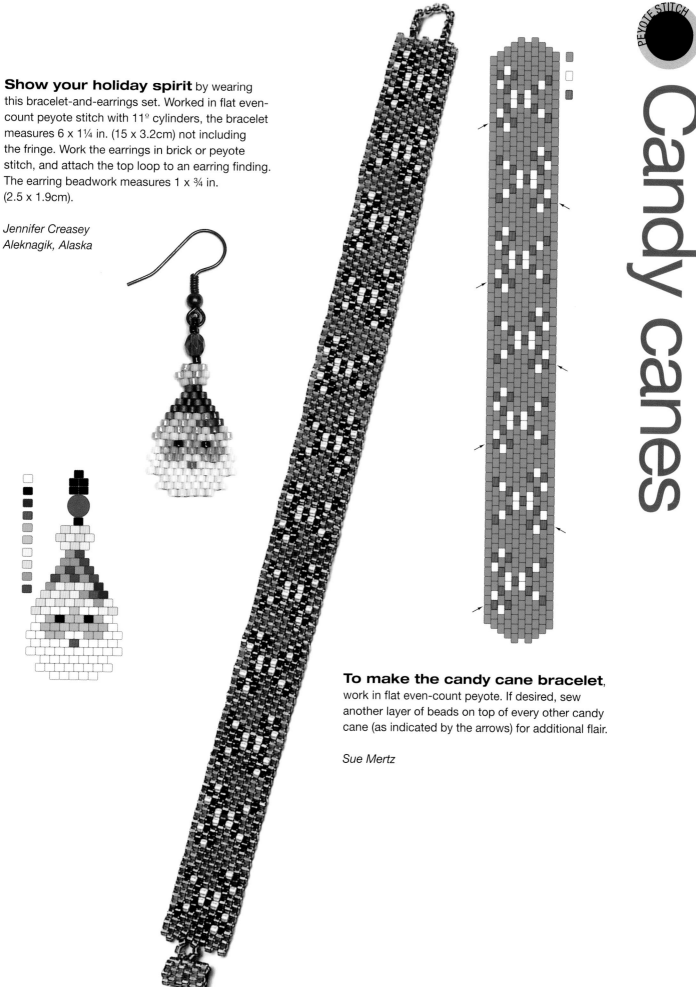

Show your holiday spirit by wearing this bracelet-and-earrings set. Worked in flat even-count peyote stitch with 11º cylinders, the bracelet measures 6 x 1¼ in. (15 x 3.2cm) not including the fringe. Work the earrings in brick or peyote stitch, and attach the top loop to an earring finding. The earring beadwork measures 1 x ¾ in. (2.5 x 1.9cm).

Jennifer Creasey
Aleknagik, Alaska

Candy canes

To make the candy cane bracelet, work in flat even-count peyote. If desired, sew another layer of beads on top of every other candy cane (as indicated by the arrows) for additional flair.

Sue Mertz

Angels

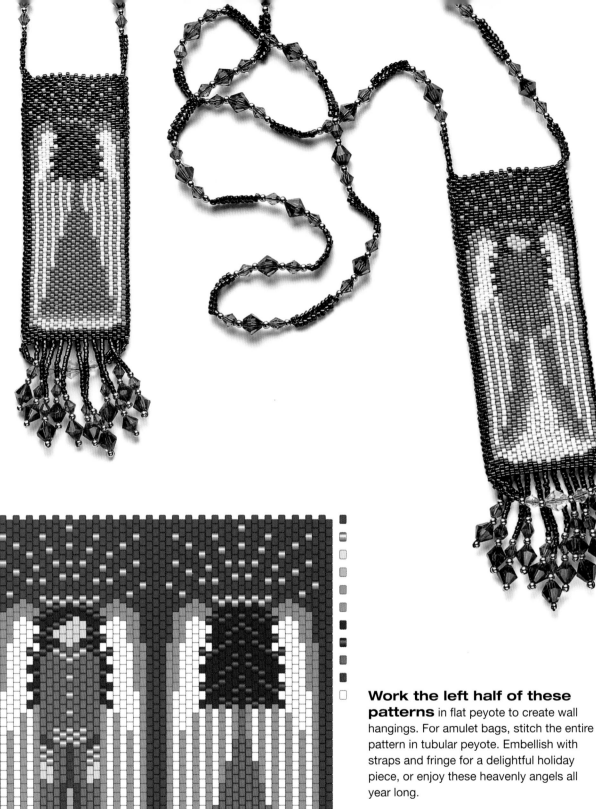

Work the left half of these patterns in flat peyote to create wall hangings. For amulet bags, stitch the entire pattern in tubular peyote. Embellish with straps and fringe for a delightful holiday piece, or enjoy these heavenly angels all year long.

Jennifer Creasey
Aleknagik, Alaska

Angels

Santa face

This jolly pattern works up quickly in two-drop peyote. Alternate silver-lined and matte beads in the red and white areas for a holiday bracelet with sparkling texture. To add edging, sew out through an edge bead, pick up two beads to match the color of the section you're edging, and sew under the adjacent thread bridge. Repeat along the length of the band and on the other side.

Jennifer Creasey
Aleknagik, Alaska

Mythological Creature Patterns

Fairy with flower

Fairy with flower

Worked in flat odd-count peyote,
this design is the perfect size for an amulet bag.

Robin Griffes
Grand Rapids, Mich.

Garden fairy

A fairy at rest in a garden

is a rare sight. Worked in flat odd-count peyote stitch, the picture measures approximately 2¾ x 3½ in. (7 x 8.9cm).

Robin Griffes
Grand Rapids, Mich.

Gryphon

Every year Amy's high school had an art contest as part of a Latin Day celebration. She designed and submitted this peyote pattern of a gryphon her freshman year.

Amy Austin
Litchfield, Conn.

Mermaid

Head for the beach with a whimsical peyote mermaid.

Robin Griffes
Grand Rapids, Mich.

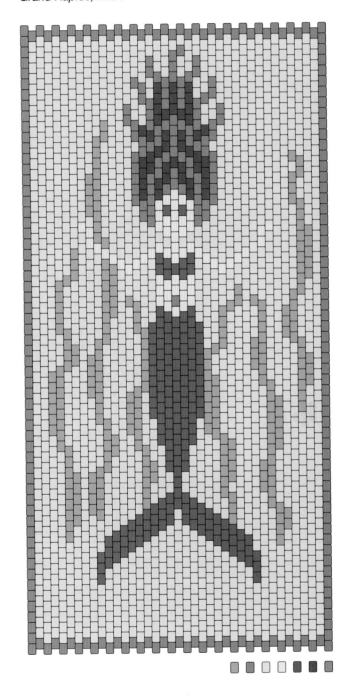

Unicorn

This amulet bag, titled "May Day," was designed for tubular brick stitch. Trudy covered each flower on the bag's front with a medium-sized five-petal glass flower in matching colors. A yellow bead at the center holds each flower in place. She also incorporated leaves and flowers into the fringe.

Trudy Merchant
Timberon, N.M.

Angels and devils

Bobbi designed this amulet bag pattern with an eye toward the dichotomy of angels vs. devils; she emphasized the contrast with her color choices.

Bobbi Bongard
New York, N.Y.

Plant, Flower, and Landscape Patterns

The great outdoors

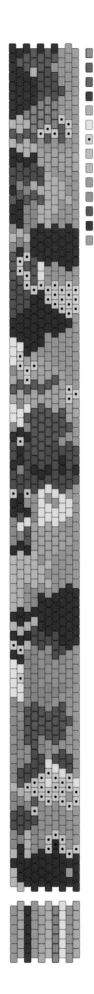

Wear this bracelet and imagine

walking through a brightly colored forest in the fall. Worked in flat even-count peyote stitch with 11º cylinder beads, the bracelet is approximately 7 in. (18cm) long. The matching toggle bar, stitched in flat peyote and zipped into a tube, is detailed at the bottom of the pattern.

Rita Grossberg
West Bloomfield, Mich.

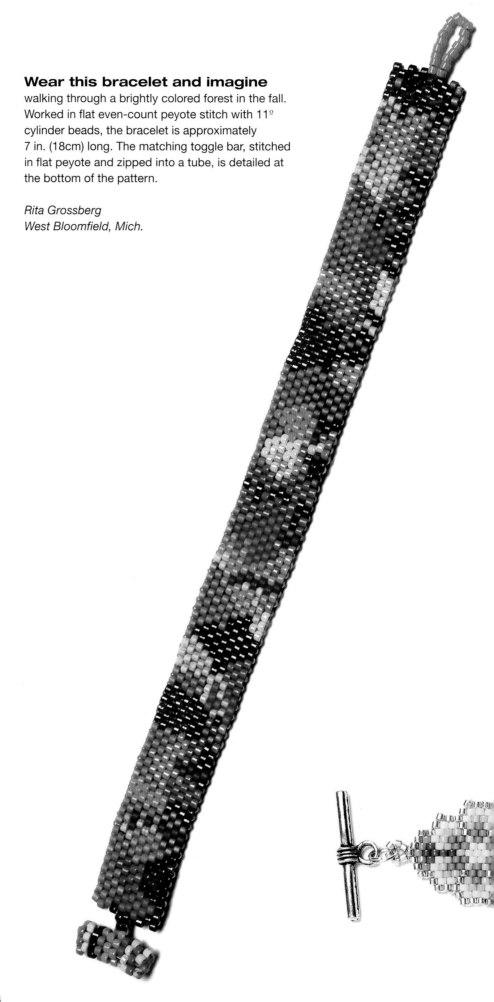

Spring flowers

A simple, cheery flower becomes the focal point for a pair of earrings and a bracelet. The flat peyote or brick stitch medallion is worked in 11º cylinder beads, starting in the center and decreasing to the tips. Add looped fringe to the beadwork at the bottom of the earrings. For the bracelet, alternate the medallions with concentric loops of cylinders.

Robin Griffes
Grand Rapids, Mich.

Daisies and roses

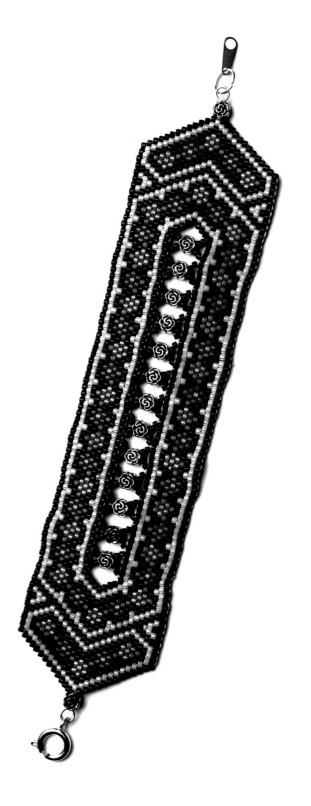

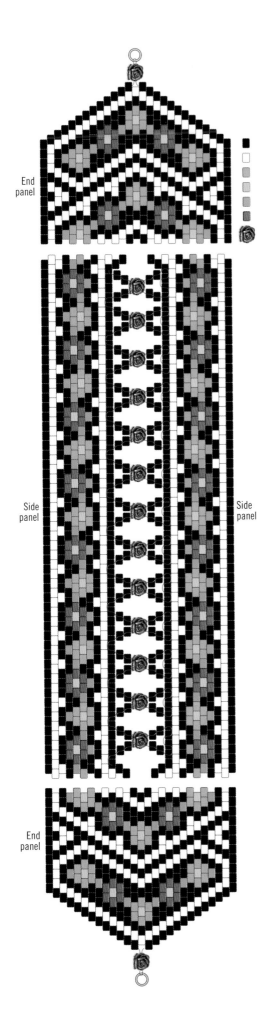

End panel

Side panel

Side panel

End panel

Working in peyote stitch, make two end panels and two side panels. Zip them up, and then add the crisscrossing motif in the center. Use soldered jump rings to attach half a clasp on each end.

Jennifer Creasey
Aleknagik, Alaska

Autumn afternoon

Maggie loves nature and spends most of her time outside. The design for her sun catcher was inspired by the tree she beads under on the shore of Lake Winnebago, Wis. The southern exposure of the sunlight at high noon is so striking that she decided to translate the colors to beads.

Maggie Beese
Oshkosh, Wis.

Out West

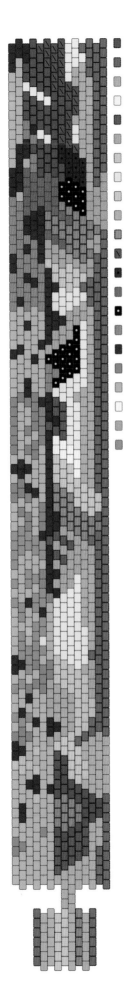

Rita is always drawing the scenery she sees when she travels. On a recent trip to the western United States, she was inspired by the colorful desert rocks and plants. This flat even-count peyote stitch bracelet measures 6¼ x ¾ in. (15.9 x 1.9cm). To make the toggle bar, work in flat peyote, and zip the ends together to form a tube.

Rita Grossberg
West Bloomfield, Mich.

A bright color palette makes Danielle's toadstool a cheerful pattern to stitch on a loom or in square stitch.

Danielle Easley
Albuquerque, N.M.

Rose barrette

When an acquaintance asked Gail to make her a barrette to match a necklace she liked to wear, Gail designed a pattern inspired by the leather buckle-like barrettes that were popular in the '70s. To leave two holes for a hairstick to hold the barrette in your hair, begin at the widest part of the pattern, and work three full-width rows. Then work 14 rows with five stitches per row to create a small tab on the left-hand side of the beadwork. Sew through the beadwork to exit the third row where the tab stops, and work 14 rows in odd-count peyote, alternating rows of 26 stitches with rows of 25 stitches. This will create the center part of the barrette. Sew through the beadwork to exit the third row where the center portion ends, and work 14 rows with five stitches per row to create the right-hand tab. Sew back to the right-hand edge of the last row stitched, and work two full-width rows to attach the loose ends of the left-hand tab, the center portion, and the right-hand tab. Work 20 decrease rows to complete the lower portion of the barrette. Add a new thread on the beginning edge, and work 20 decrease rows to complete the upper portion. Add fringe in varying lengths across the bottom of the barrette.

Gail Ainsworth/Krutka
Wendell, Mass.

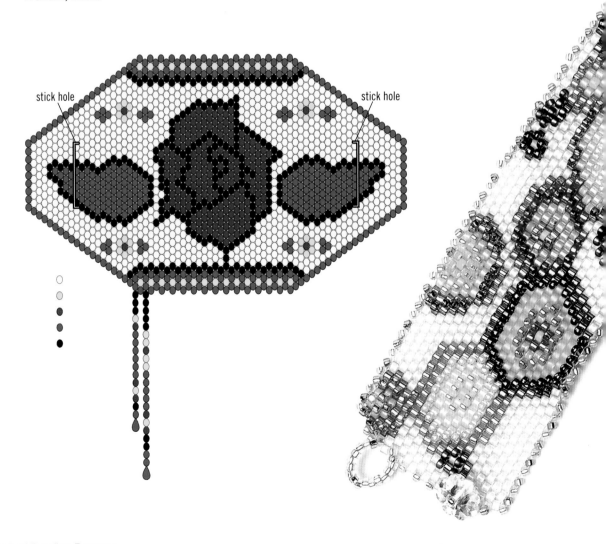

stick hole   stick hole

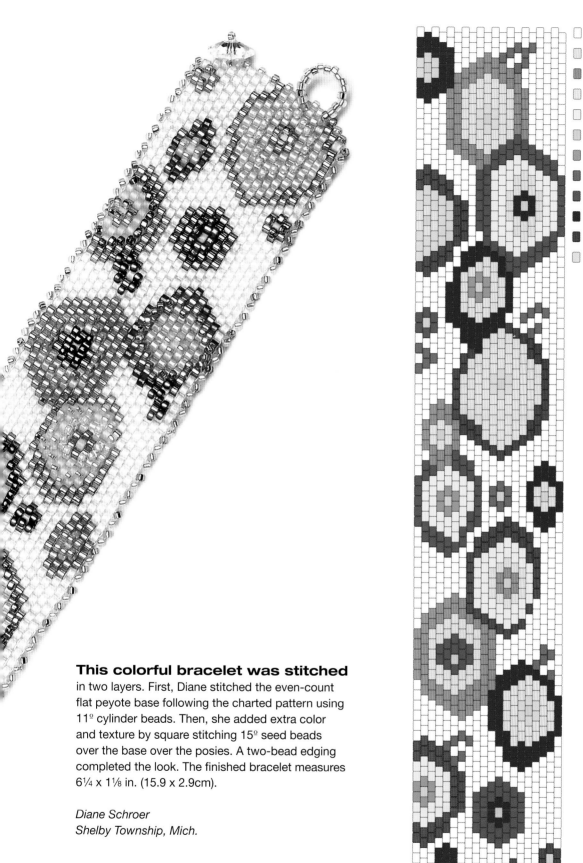

Pocket of posies

This colorful bracelet was stitched
in two layers. First, Diane stitched the even-count
flat peyote base following the charted pattern using
11° cylinder beads. Then, she added extra color
and texture by square stitching 15° seed beads
over the base over the posies. A two-bead edging
completed the look. The finished bracelet measures
$6\frac{1}{4}$ x $1\frac{1}{8}$ in. (15.9 x 2.9cm).

Diane Schroer
Shelby Township, Mich.

Summer gardens

With the colorful landscape of this peyote band, you can wear the cheer of a summer garden around your wrist anytime. The matching toggle bar is stitched in flat peyote and the ends are zipped together to form a tube.

Rita Grossberg
West Bloomfield, Mich.

Bouquet earrings

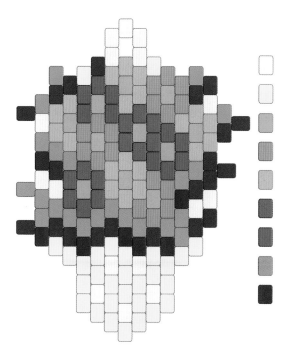

This pattern makes a great base for earrings. The stitching is quick, and you can get creative when you choose the beads to use in the long fringe.

Jennifer Creasey
Aleknagik, Alaska

Flower garden bag

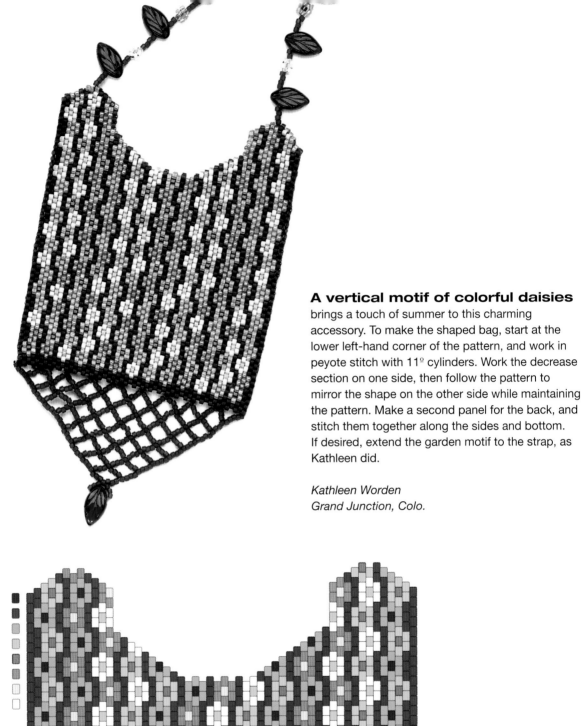

A vertical motif of colorful daisies brings a touch of summer to this charming accessory. To make the shaped bag, start at the lower left-hand corner of the pattern, and work in peyote stitch with 11º cylinders. Work the decrease section on one side, then follow the pattern to mirror the shape on the other side while maintaining the pattern. Make a second panel for the back, and stitch them together along the sides and bottom. If desired, extend the garden motif to the strap, as Kathleen did.

Kathleen Worden
Grand Junction, Colo.

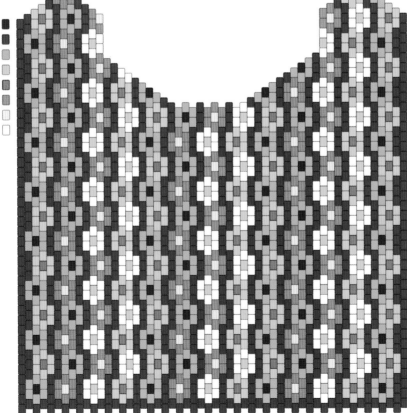

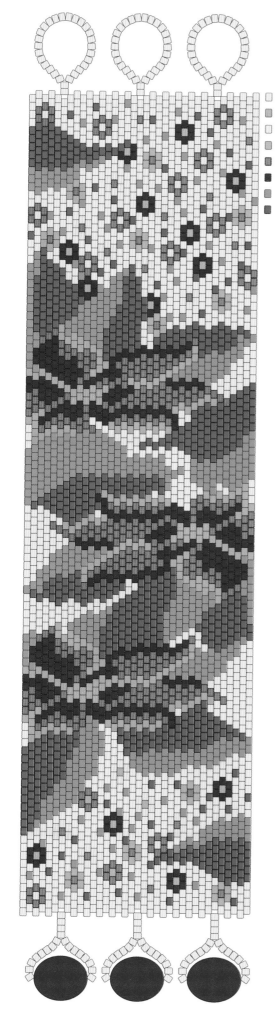

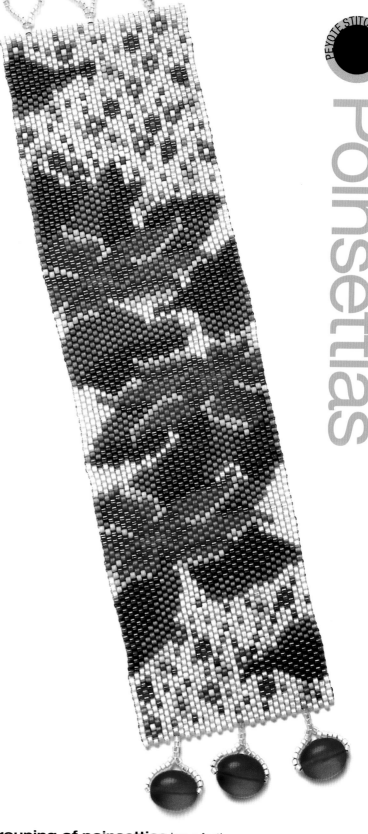

Poinsettias

A grouping of poinsettias has a festive holiday look, but the dainty flowers and gold-tone background make this lush bracelet appealing year-round. The extra-wide band is worked in flat even-count peyote stitch with 11º cylinders and measures 7½ x 1⅞ in. (19.1 x 4.8cm).

Robin Griffes
Grand Rapids, Mich.

Flower vases

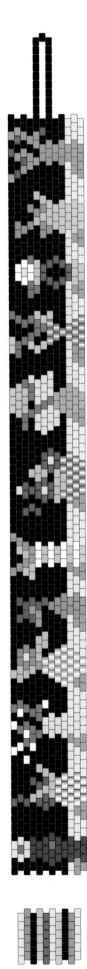

Rita imagined a dark winter day

brightened by a windowsill full of cut flowers for this peyote stitch bracelet, earrings, and pendant. The bracelet clasp is a peyote stitch strip zipped into a tube with a seed bead loop. The bracelet is approximately 7 in. (18cm) long. Small loops on the tops of the earrings and pendant attach to an earring finding or jump ring. The earrings and pendant are also embellished with cylinder beads to create three-dimensional flowers.

Rita Grossberg
West Bloomfield, Mich.

Cherokee Rose

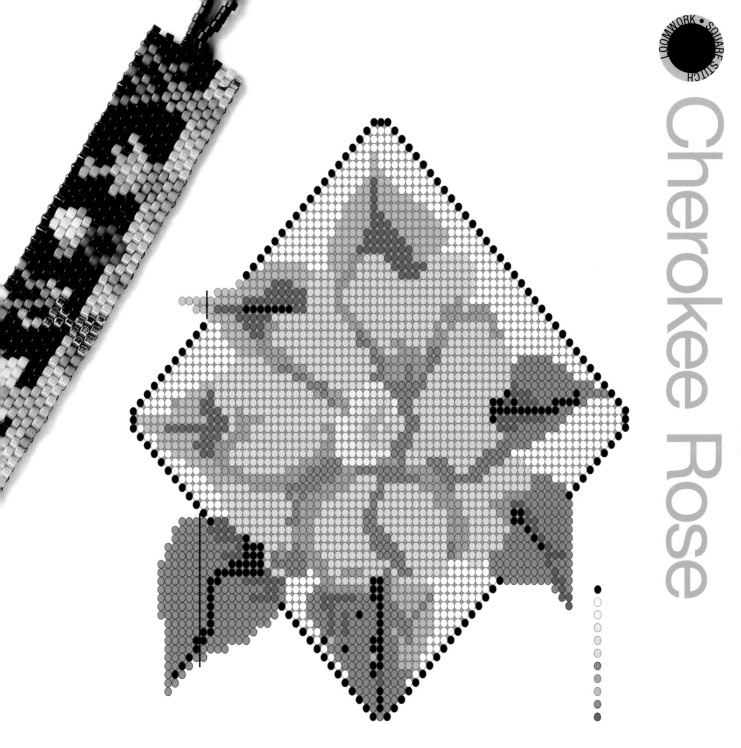

This loomwork pattern was inspired by the legend of the beautiful Cherokee Rose that grows along the Trail of Tears. According to legend, the Cherokee elders prayed for a sign to lift the spirits of the grieving mothers and give them strength to care for their children. From that day forward, a beautiful rose grew wherever a mother's tear fell to the ground. The leaves on the left side of the pattern are worked in square stitch. Each leaf has a line marked on the pattern to separate the square stitch sections from the loomwork.

Lois A. Fetters
White Cloud, Mich.

Adirondacks

Devin designed this flat peyote pattern for an amulet bag with help from her best friend and her daughter. She enjoys wearing it as a necklace because she can reverse the sides to show when day turns to night. The bag is accented with small bird, bear, and fish beads as befit this wilderness landscape.

Devin LaFave
Tupper Lake, N.Y.

Strawberries

Melissa made this peyote stitch pattern for her young daughters, who love strawberry short-cake as much as she did when she was their age. You can choose a variety of background colors to complement the berries and leaves. The finished work measures 1¾ in. (4.4cm) square.

*Melissa Johnson
Blanchard, Mich.*

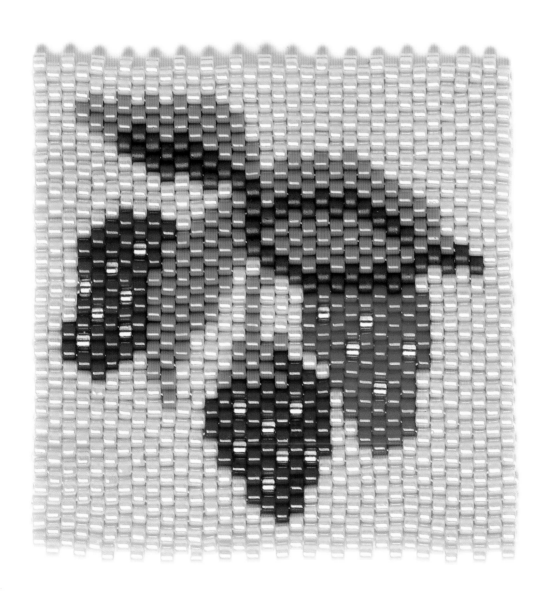

Daisy band

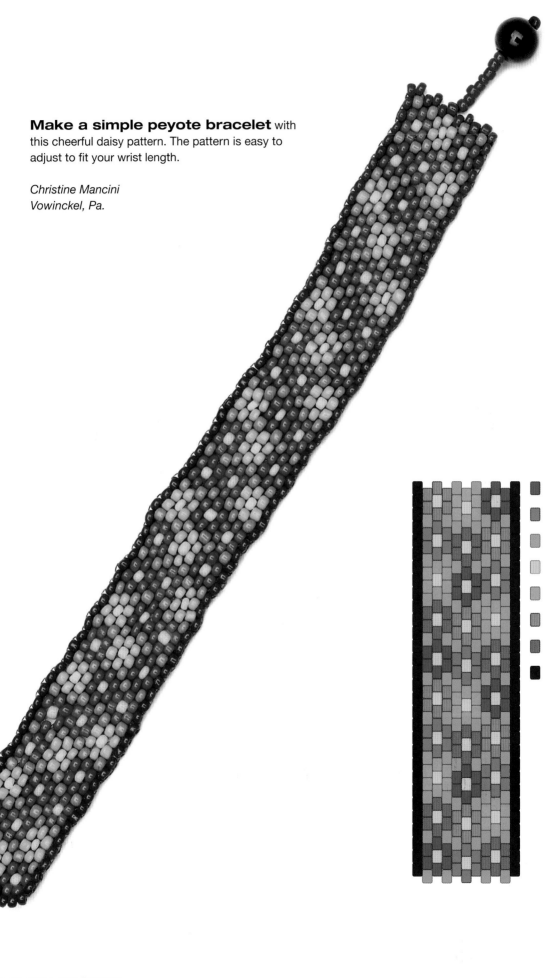

Make a simple peyote bracelet with this cheerful daisy pattern. The pattern is easy to adjust to fit your wrist length.

Christine Mancini
Vowinckel, Pa.

Miscellaneous Patterns

Gauguin paintings

A trip to Tahiti inspired Claire to design two amulet bag patterns based on paintings by French Post-Impressionist artist Paul Gauguin. The pattern on this page is based on *Tahitian Woman with Blossom*, while the pattern on p. 109 is inspired by *When Are You Getting Married?*

Claire Laufman
Huntington, N.Y.

Gauguin paintings

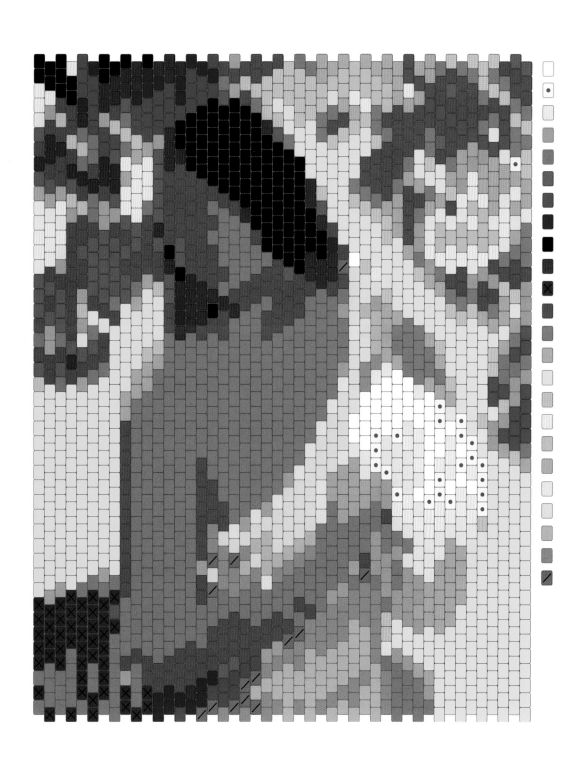

Circus clowns

These patterns for a bracelet, earrings, and amulet bag bring the circus to life. The pieces are stitched using 11º cylinder beads. The bracelet, measuring 1½ x 7 in. (3.8 x 18cm), is edged with 4mm Swarovski pearls. The toggle is a 6mm Swarovski pearl that slips through a loop. The amulet bag is zipped up on one side and stitched together on the bottom edge. The fringe also uses 4mm and 6mm Swarovski pearls. The earrings can be sewn in either brick or peyote stitch. The top loop on the earring attaches to an earring finding.

Jennifer Creasey
Aleknagik, Alaska

Circus clowns

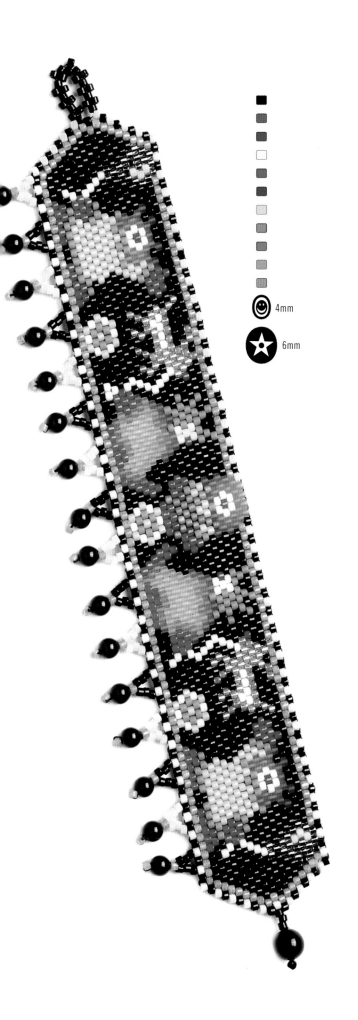

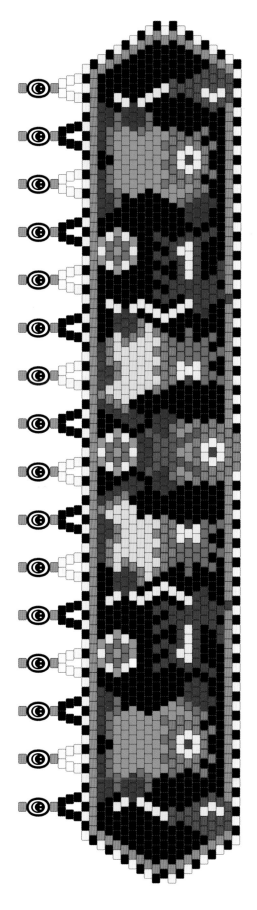

4mm

6mm

Mona Lisa

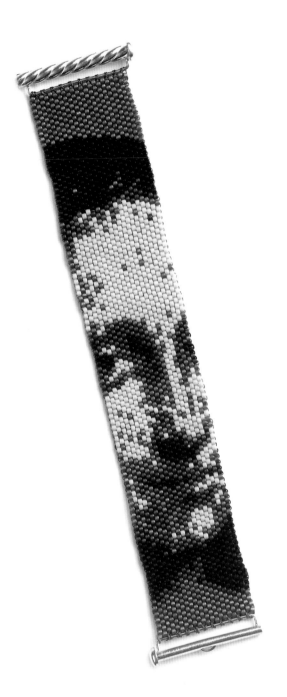

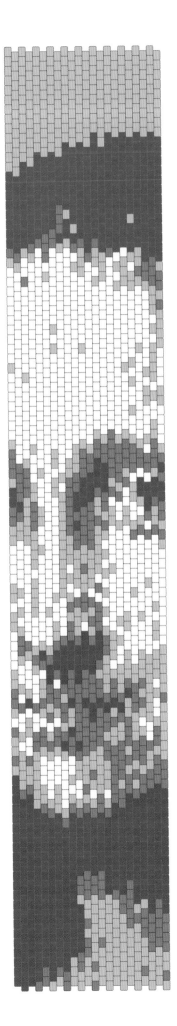

When Diane designed this pattern, she wanted an effect similar to turn-of-the-century sepia photos. She used matte black, matte ivory, matte bronze, and matte olive-rose beads, and sewed the flat even-count peyote stitch panel to a silver slide clasp.

Diana Hiott
Montgomery, Ala.

Southwestern motif

**Antonio created this design for
a Native American friend** to attach
to his billfold. The deer's skull is a common
Southwestern image, and the gourd rattle is used
in Native American ceremonies. He used 11º seed
beads in opaque white, gray, orange, yellow, red,
and matte black, and worked the piece in flat odd-
count peyote stitch.

Antonio A. Calles
Soledad, Calif.

Alphabet pendants

Wendy designed this alphabet for a beading class she taught at the Anderson Ranch Arts Center in Snowmass, Colo. Her students, aged 9 to 13, beaded the initials of their first, middle, and last names. Wendy stitched the multicolored samples to show how different colors look next to each other and to demonstrate various fringe options. This helped the students make their own color selections and embellish the letters.

Wendy Ellsworth
Quakertown, Pa.

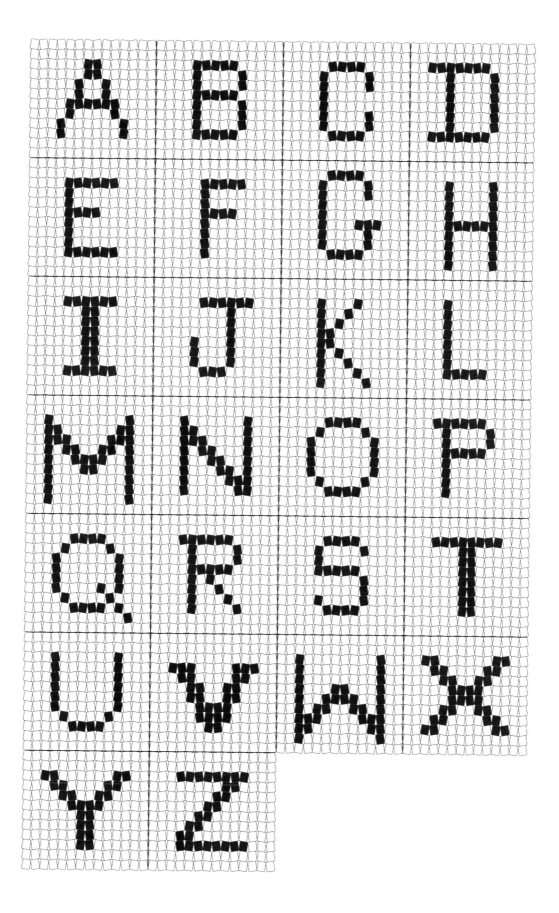

House amulet

This amulet bag features three-dimensional construction. Windows on one side of the bag open to a flower garden, and French doors on the other side open to a grassy meadow.

Stephanie Trice
Houston, Texas

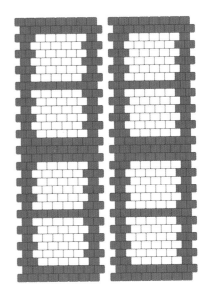

Windows

First, make the window frame, flower scene, and window panes in brick stitch. To work the frame, start at the bottom and complete the first six rows. Continue working from the bottom up and complete the left side to the top of the window frame. Then work the right side from the bottom of the window frame up. Connect the two sides with the top six rows. Assemble the pieces: Position the flower scene behind the window frame so it is centered in the opening and sew the two panels together. Sew through the up-beads and whip stitch a window panel to each side of the opening on the frame to create a hinge so the windows open.

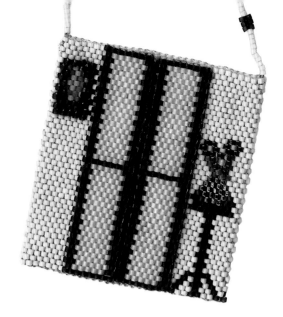

House amulet

French doors

Work this side of the bag and the doors in brick stitch. Whip stitch the doors over the meadow scene so they line up when closed. Sew the two sides of the bag together, and add a strap.

Beaded wristwatches

You can permanently set these watches for your favorite time of day. To simulate a black lizard skin band, alternate matte black beads with opaque black beads (indicated by the black and gray colors in the pattern). The gold-band pattern creates the look of a diamond-studded band. For both bracelets, Ellen sandwiched a brass bracelet blank between the beadwork and a strip of Ultrasuede. She sewed the edges together, then embellished them with triangle beads. Ellen used a Czech fire-polished bead and an 11º for each watch stem.

Ellen Friedenberg
New York, N.Y.

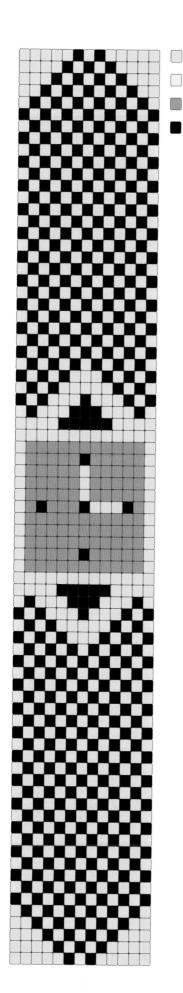

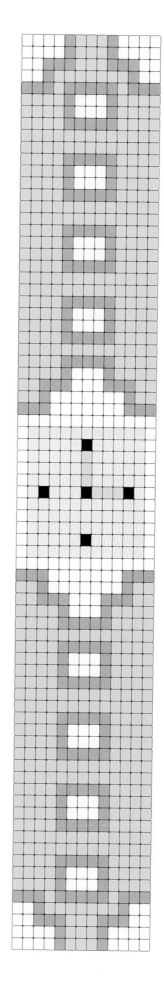

Beaded wristwatches

Caribbean cruise

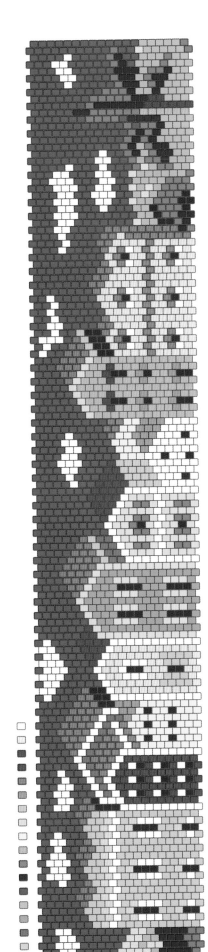

Rita and Julie, a mother-and-daughter beading team, were inspired by the Caribbean island of Curaçao. The island's colorful multistory buildings, sparkling water, bright sunshine, and tropical trees are all captured in these designs. Rita visited the island on a cruise and transferred a photo she took of the local architecture onto graph paper. Her bracelet pattern is an extended view of the waterfront, with a lone palm tree standing proudly on the beach. She stitched her bracelet in flat even-count peyote. It measures 7 x 1⅜ in. (18 x 3.5cm). Julie stitched the business card holder in flat odd-count peyote with the same design on both sides, zipping up the edges on three sides to form the holder that measures 4 x 2½ in. (10 x 6.4cm).

Rita Grossberg
West Bloomfield, Mich.

Julie Glasser
Alpharetta, Ga.

Caribbean cruise

Piano keys

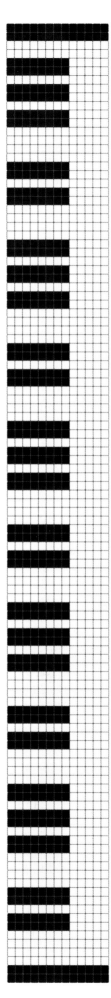

Music fans will love this multi-octave keyboard. You can make the bracelet longer or shorter by adding or omitting keys. A one-octave length would be suitable for a pin. The square stitch rows are added lengthwise, rather than across the band. This positions the thread between the beads so that you can use a fine-point marker wih permanent black ink to define the keys. To do this, fold the keyboard to expose the thread between the black beads, and color the thread between the black beads to make the two black rows look like one key. To define the white keys, color the thread between every third row of white beads. A simple loop and button clasp completes the bracelet.

David Farnsworth
Rochester, N.Y.

Puzzle pieces

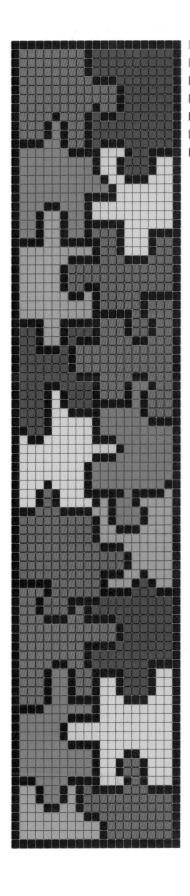

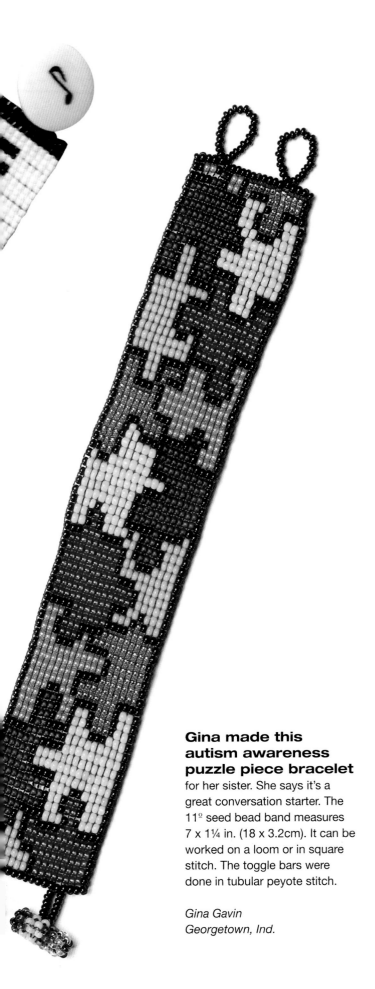

Gina made this autism awareness puzzle piece bracelet for her sister. She says it's a great conversation starter. The 11º seed bead band measures 7 x 1¼ in. (18 x 3.2cm). It can be worked on a loom or in square stitch. The toggle bars were done in tubular peyote stitch.

Gina Gavin
Georgetown, Ind.

Sci-fi filmstrip

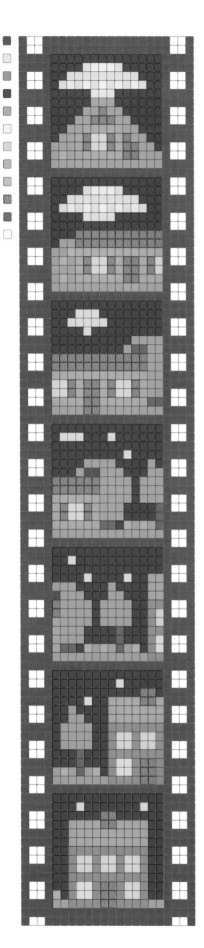

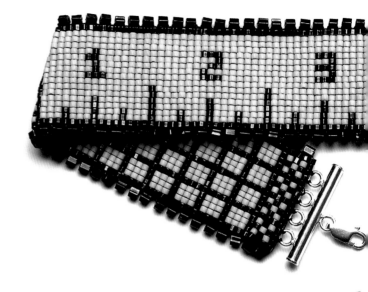

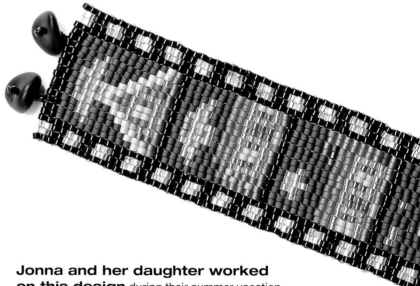

Jonna and her daughter worked on this design during their summer vacation. It reminds them of their favorite science fiction movies — the Martians always seem to land on quiet summer nights. The bracelet is 7¼ in. (18.4cm) long.

Jonna Ellis Holston
Kernersville, N.C.

Ruler

To make this playful choker, begin with the ruler portion, and then stitch the repeating grid pattern at the ends to the desired length. Ellen used cylinder beads in iris-finished blue-black and matte cream, and attached a sterling silver clasp. She finished the edges with 10° triangle beads that matched the dark cylinders.

Ellen Friedenberg
New York, N.Y.

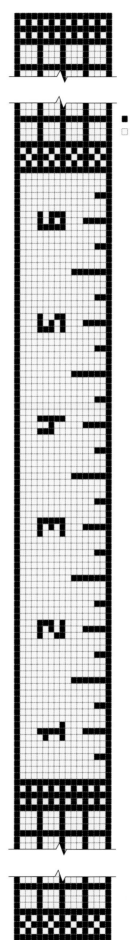

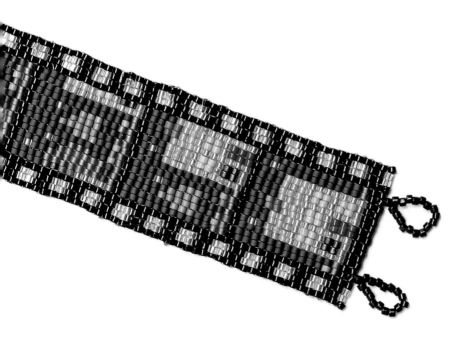

Manhattan skyline

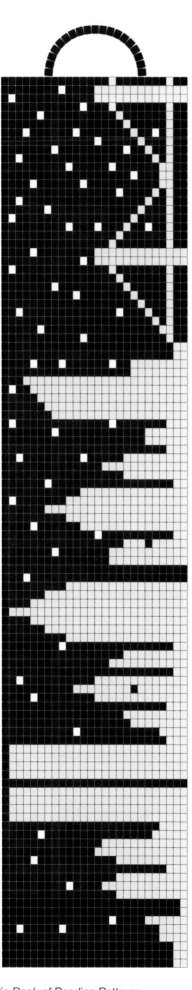

Irene is a native New Yorker but has lived in California for 19 years. Her family has visited Manhattan many times, and she taught her children the names of her favorite skyscrapers. She designed this bracelet after a visit to New York in July 2001. "Soon after I completed stitching the bracelet," she says, "the twin towers of the World Trade Center were gone and the physical and emotional landscape of my hometown was changed forever." Irene has kept this design as a memorial to a time and place altered by the tragedy. The bracelet is sewn using black, gray, and crystal cylinder beads with a picot edging of black cylinders and silver Charlottes.
It measures 7 x 1½ in. (18 x 3.8cm).

Irene Landaw
Castro Valley, Calif.

There are more than 100 manned lighthouses in the state of Michigan. Many are open to the public, but some are in disrepair or abandoned. Lois's daughter and son-in-law are intrigued by these lighthouses and are determined to see every one. With them in mind, she created this pattern for the loom.

Lois A. Fetters
White Cloud, Mich.

PEYOTE STITCH

Photo-frame pendant

Hold your loved ones close to your heart with a charming picture frame pendant. Working in peyote stitch, begin at the bottom left-hand corner of panel A. Continue along the left-hand side with panel B. Using a new thread, add panel C. Flip the piece over, and add panels D and E. Make panels F and G separately, then attach them as shown. When the entire piece is complete, fold it in half, stitch the sides together, and add decorative edging. Add fringe between the beads of the bottom row as shown, and string or stitch a neck strap.

Jennifer Creasey
Aleknagik, Alaska

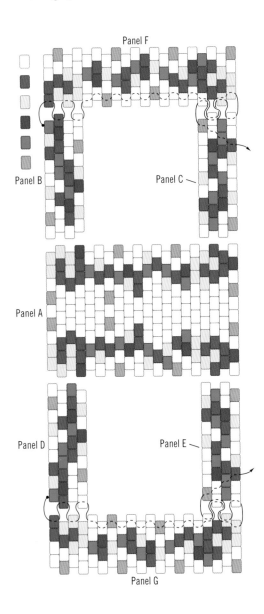

Panel F

Panel B

Panel C

Panel A

Panel D

Panel E

Panel G

Red hat

Make a simple peyote bracelet

as a salute to Red Hat Ladies everywhere by repeating this red hat pattern over and over for the desired length.

Christine Mancini
Vowinckel, Pa.

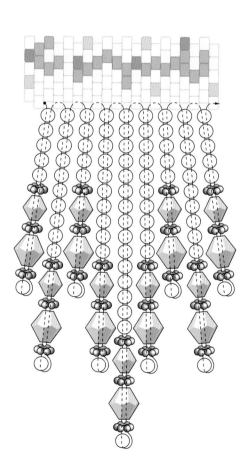

Burning candle

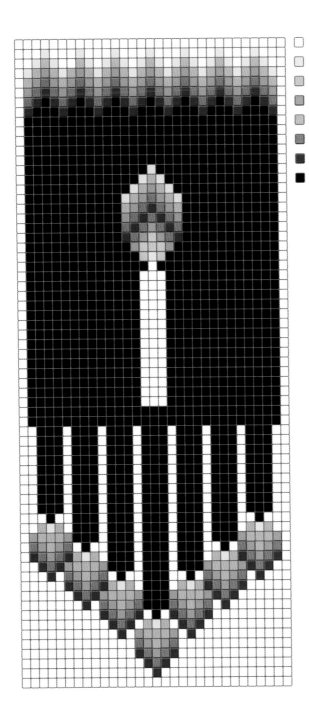

This bold amulet bag design looks great in square stitch or loomwork. Use round seed beads or cylinder beads. It's up to you.

Giuseppe Chemello
Torre Balfredo, Italy

PEYOTE STITCH • LOOMW
NE STITCH • RIGHT ANGLE WEAV
CH • LOOMWORK • SQUARE STITCH
GHT ANGLE WEAVE • BRICK STITCH • PEYOT
WORK • SQUARE STITCH • HERRINGBONE STITCH
WEAVE • BRICK STITCH • PEYOTE STITCH • LOOM
RE STITCH • RIGHT ANGLE WEAVE • HERRINGBONE S
HT ANGLE WEAVE • BRICK STITCH • PEYOTE STITCH • L
RK • SQUARE STITCH • HERRINGBONE STITCH • RIGHT
WEAVE • BRICK STITCH • PEYOTE STITCH • LOOMWORK
ARE STITCH • HERRINGBONE STITCH • RIGHT ANGLE W
K STITCH • PEYOTE STITCH • LOOMWORK • SQUARE
RRINGBONE STITCH • RIGHT ANGLE WEAVE • BRICK
E STITCH • LOOMWORK • SQUARE STITCH • LO
GBONE STITCH • RIGHT ANGLE WEAVE • BRI
CH • LOOMWORK • SQUARE STITCH•
WEAVE • BRICK STITCH • PEYO
STITCH • HERRINGB

Bonus Projects

Loominosity

Construct a glowing beaded lantern, panel by panel

designed by **Naomi Sakuma**

Loominosity

FIGURE 1

This brilliant lantern designed by Naomi Sakuma is a true work of art. Patterns for four panels, each representing a season, are here, as well as dragonfly, snowflake, and ladybug embellishments. Instructions for attaching the panels to a frame and a few ideas for displaying your handiwork are also included.

step by step

Loom setup

The beading loom we used to make the panels is 24 x 8 in. (61 x 20cm). The beaded panels measure 13½ x 6½ in. (34.3 x 16.5cm). The bugle beads at the top and bottom of each pattern are pre-strung as you warp the loom.

[1] Make a loop at the center of 8 yd. (7.3m) of thread, and tie it around the first pin, screw, or hook on the loom.
[2] Attach a needle to the end of one of the 4-yd. (3.7m) threads. Place the thread in the first open slot of the warp guide, pick up two bugle beads, and place the thread in the first slot on the opposite side. Wrap the thread around the pin on

this side of the loom, place the thread in the next slot of the warp guide, and sew back through the bugles. Place the thread in the next slot of the warp guide on the first side, and wrap the thread around the first pin. Repeat for a second set of warp threads. Tie the thread to the pin (figure 1).
[3] Repeat step 2 to add two more sets of warp threads with the remaining 4-yd. (3.7m) thread.
[4] Maintaining even tension, repeat steps 1–3 until you have 116 warp threads, switching to the pin, screw or hook that lines up best with the area of the loom as you work across the loom.

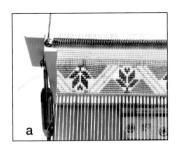

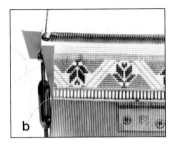

Border
DB-0762 Matte opaque dark cream ☐
DB-0042 Transparent silver lined gold ▨
DB-0115 Dark topaz gold luster ☐
DB-0327 Matte metallic dark green iris ▪

Winter
DB-6050 Crystal luster ☐
DB-0113 Transparent blue luster ☐
DB-0312 Matte metallic copper ▪
DB-0378 Matte metallic brick red ▪
DB-0915 Sparkle ginger lined crystal ◨
DB-0101 Light smoky topaz luster ▨

Spring
DB-0706 Transparent aqua ☐
DB-0312 Matte metallic copper ▪
DB-0062 Light cranberry lined topaz luster ▨
DB-0903 Sparkle celery lined crystal ☐
DB-0152 Transparent green AB ▨

Summer
DB-0109 Crystal ivory gold luster ☐
DB-0174 Transparent chartreuse AB ▨
DB-0152 Transparent green AB ▨
DB-0175 Transparent emerald AB ▪
DB-0022L Light bronze ▨
DB-0327 Matte metallic dark green iris ▪
DB-0312 Matte metallic copper ▪

Autumn
DB-0109 Crystal ivory gold luster ☐
DB-0852 Matte cantaloupe AB ▨
DB-0272 Goldenrod lined topaz AB ▨
DB-0913 Sparkle salmon lined topaz ▨
DB-0022L Light bronze ▨
DB-0312 Matte metallic copper ▪
DB-0111 Transparent blue gray rainbow gold luster ☐
DB-0059 Amethyst lined crystal AB ▨
DB-0601 Dyed silver lined burnt orange ▪
DB-0242 Silver gray Ceylon ☐

Sun
DB-0762 Matte opaque dark cream ☐
DB-0075 Dark coral lined crystal AB ▨
DB-0043 Silver lined flame red ▨
DB-0295 Lined red AB ▪
DB-0603 Dyed silver lined brick red ▨

FIGURE 2

FIGURE 3

Patterns

Work the panels using the color keys provided or the colors of your choice.

[1] Tie a comfortable length of thread to the top of the left-most warp thread. Using matte opaque dark cream cylinders, work five rows of loomwork (Basics, p. 5) at the top of the loom. These rows will be used to attach the panel to the frame.

[2] Following the pattern in **figure 2**, work the first 18 rows (beginning with the top border of the pattern, above the bugles). Slide the bugles up to the 18th row **(photo a)**, and resume the pattern below the bugles **(photo b)**. End and add thread as needed (Basics). When you've finished the body of the pattern, slide the second set of bugles up to the last row worked, and finish the last 18 rows of the border. Work five more rows in matte opaque dark cream cylinders.

[3] Remove the panel from the loom by carefully cutting the warp threads as close to the pin, screw, or hook as possible, as you will be using the warp threads to attach the panel to the frame. Set this panel aside.

[4] Repeat steps 1–3 three times, following the patterns in **figures 3, 4, and 5.**

EDITOR'S NOTES:
• The lantern frames pictured are hand-crafted. Place orders through metiers.biz, and allow at least six weeks for delivery. The frames cost about $140.00 USD.
• The lantern frame has a place to attach a lighting kit, which can be found at most hardware stores. Use a maximum of a 20-watt bulb.
• As you work, use a guide to mark your place on the pattern.
• To view and print larger versions of the loom patterns and Naomi's color chart, go to the June and August 2008 Resource Guide at BeadAndButton.com. While there, you can also watch videos showing how to assemble the lantern.
• Use dowels to hang all four panels for a wall decoration.
• Separate each season, the border, and the sun into different trays to make it easy to transition and keep track of colors.

LOOMWORK

Dragonfly

[1] Cut a 24-in. (61cm) piece of 28-gauge craft wire, and work in crossweave technique (Basics) following figure 6 to make the head of the dragonfly. Use the two 4–6mm round beads for the dragonfly's eyes.

[2] With the remaining wire ends, attach the head of the dragonfly to the loom panel above the body (photo c).

[3] Refer to figure 7 to construct two sets of dragonfly wings in square stitch (Basics).

[4] Cut a 10-in. (25cm) piece of 28-gauge wire, run it through the outside edge of the wings, and attach the wings to the loom panel, next to the body (photo d).

FIGURE 6

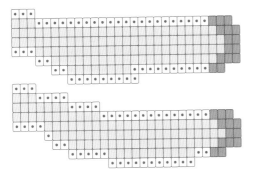

FIGURE 7

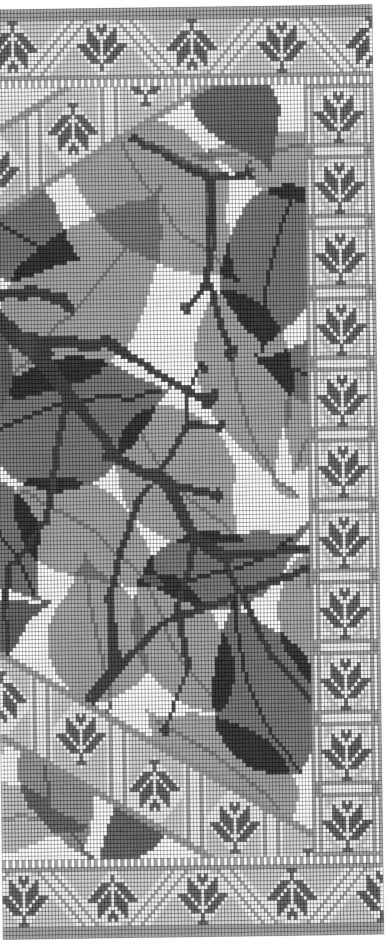

FIGURE 4

FIGURE 5

Snowflake

[1] On 1 yd. (.9m) of thread, pick up six 4mm bicone crystals, leaving a 6-in. (15cm) tail. Sew through the first 4mm again to form a ring (**figure 8, a–b**). Pick up a 4mm, and sew through the opposite 4mm in the ring (**b–c**).

[2] Pick up two cylinders, a 4mm, and a cylinder. Sew through the first cylinder again and continue through the next 4mm in the ring (**figure 9**). Repeat around the ring.

[3] Retrace the thread path, but do not trim the working thread or tail.

[4] Using the working thread and tail, attach the snowflake to the circle of clear beads in the upper left-hand corner of the winter panel (**photo e**). Secure the working thread and tail with a few half-hitch knots (Basics), and trim.

FIGURE 8

FIGURE 9

Finishing

[1] Measure the body of the panels between the two rows of bugle beads, and cut two pieces of interfacing to fit just inside those measurements. Align each piece of interfacing with the surface of the panel that will face the inside of the lantern. Whip stitch (Basics) the interfacing to the edge warp thread.

[2] Use comfortable lengths of metallic thread and sewing needles to top-stitch along the outlines of the borders, leaves, and other points of interest on the panels (**photo f**).

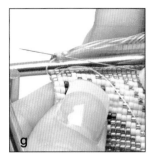

FIGURE 10

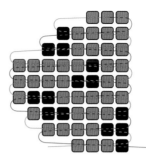

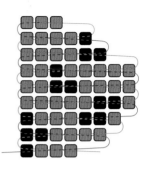

FIGURE 11

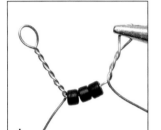

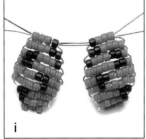

Frame

[1] Lay the first panel on a flat surface, with the interfacing facing up. Lay the frame on its side on top of the panel. Fold the first few rows of the panel over the top bar of the frame, and using the warp threads and a square stitch thread path, stitch the first row of matte opaque dark cream cylinders to the third row of the border pattern **(photo g)**.

[2] Work in all the warp threads, securing the panel to the frame. Be careful not to fill up the cylinders with thread before using all the warp tails. Secure the warp tails, and trim.

[3] Repeat on the other end of the panel, attaching it to the bottom bar of the frame.

[4] Repeat steps 1–3 with the remaining panels.

Ladybug

[1] Cut a 12-in. (30cm) piece of 28-gauge craft wire, and work in cross-weave technique (Basics) following **figure 10** to make the body of the ladybug, starting with the antennae **(photo h)**. Do not trim the wire tails.

[2] Refer to **figure 11** to make two wings, attach them to each other **(photo i)**, and then to the body with a pair of wires **(photo j)**. Weave that set of wires along the edge of the wings, and trim.

[3] Use the two wire tails from the body and the two wires from the wings to attach the ladybug to the lantern frame **(photo k)**.

[4] Repeat steps 1–3 to make a second ladybug.

materials

**loomwork panel lamp
with four 13½ x 6½-in.
(34.3 x 16.5cm) panels**

- **928** 6mm Japanese bugle beads
- **18** 4mm bicone crystals
- **2** 4–6mm round beads
- 11º Japanese cylinder beads, in each of **28** colors:
  3g per dragonfly color
  2g per ladybug color
  30–40g per season and sun color
  100–150g per border color
- 2 yd. (1.8m) 28-gauge craft wire
- nylon beading thread
- spool of metallic thread
- extra long beading needles, #12
- sewing needles
- large beading loom
- ¼-yd. (23cm) medium-weight interfacing for lining the panels
- lantern frame (See Editor's Notes for more information)
- wire cutters

See p. 134 for a complete list of cylinder bead colors.

Victorian spirit

Whether loomwoven or square stitched, these patterned panels connected by beaded strands make a great ensemble.

designed by **Jennifer Creasey**

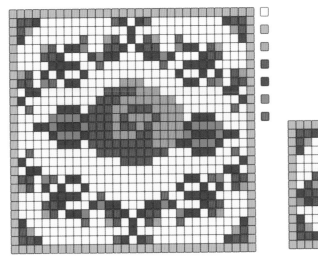

FIGURE 1   FIGURE 2

materials

necklace 36 in. (.9m)

- **16** 7 x 11mm teardrop-shaped crystals
- **43** 6mm bicone crystals
- **70** 4mm bicone crystals
- **242** 3mm round gold-colored beads
- Japanese cylinder beads
  20g cream, color A
  5g gold, color B
  5g rose, color C
  5g dark rose, color D
  3g dark green, color E
  2g green, color F
  1g fuchsia, color G
- nylon beading thread
- beading needles, #12
- beading loom (optional)

earrings

- **6** 7 x 11mm teardrop-shaped crystals
- **6** 6mm bicone crystals
- **6** 4mm bicone crystals
- **30** 3mm round gold-colored beads
- Japanese cylinder beads
  2g cream, color A
  2g gold, color B
  1g rose, color C
  1g dark rose, color D
  1g dark green, color E
  1g green, color F
- pair of earring findings
- nylon beading thread
- beading needles, #12
- beading loom (optional)
- chainnose pliers

step by step

Necklace

The rose-pattern panels can be made on a loom or in square stitch. Refer to either the Loomwork or Square stitch section of Basics, p. 5, before you begin.

Centerpiece panel

Thread a needle on 1 yd. (.9m) of thread. If using a loom, set it up with 32 warp threads, and tie the 1-yd. (.9m) working thread to the first warp, leaving a 6-in. (15cm) tail. If using square stitch, pick up a stop bead (Basics), leaving a 6-in. (15cm) tail.

Follow the pattern in **figure 1** to make one panel using cylinder beads. Remove the stop bead (if working in square stitch) or cut the panel from the loom, weave the tails or warp threads into the beadwork, and trim.

Strap panels

Make a total of eight strap panels as follows:

If using a loom, set it up with 11 warp threads. Following the pattern in **figure 2**, weave each panel from top to bottom, and leave a 16-in. (41cm) tail at the lower right-hand corner. Secure the beginning tail in the beadwork, and trim. Weave the warp threads into the beadwork to secure them, and trim.

If using square stitch, stitch each panel from top to bottom, and leave a 16-in. (41cm) tail at the lower right-hand

corner. Remove the stop bead, secure the beginning tail in the beadwork, and trim.

Strap

[1] Thread a needle on the 16-in. (41cm) tail at the bottom of one strap panel. Sew through the second-to-last row, then sew through the edge bead of the first row (figure 3, a–b).

[2] Pick up a 3mm gold bead, ten color A cylinder beads, a 3mm, a 4mm bicone crystal, a 3mm, a 6mm bicone crystal, a 3mm, a 4mm, a 3mm, ten As, and a 3mm (b–c). Sew into the centerpiece panel at the edge, sew through two beads in the second row, and sew through the adjacent bead in the first row (c–d).

[3] Sew through the 3mm, then pick up ten As (d–e). Sew through the next seven beads (e–f). Pick up ten As, and sew through the first 3mm picked up (f–g).

[4] Sew into the strap panel between the two beads you exited, and sew through the next four edge beads (g–h).

[5] Make two more connecting strands (h–i). Secure the thread in the beadwork with half-hitch knots, and trim.

[6] Repeat steps 1–5, joining the remaining seven strap panels to each other. Then attach the final strap panel to the other side of the centerpiece in the same way.

Fringe

[1] To make the fringe, secure 2 yd. (1.8m) of thread near the bottom of the centerpiece. Sew through the

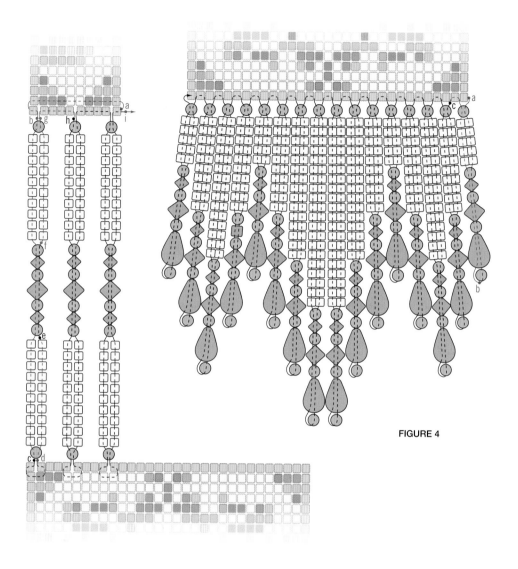

FIGURE 3

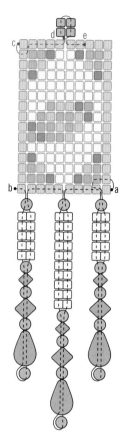

FIGURE 4

FIGURE 5

beadwork, and exit an edge bead on the bottom row.

[2] Pick up a 3mm, five As, a 3mm, a 4mm, a 3mm, a 6mm, a 3mm, a teardrop-shaped crystal, and a 3mm (figure 4, a–b). Skip the 3mm, and sew back through the next six beads. Pick up five As, sew through the next 3mm, and sew through the second edge bead (b–c). Continue adding fringe across the bottom row as shown in figure 4. Secure the tail, and trim.

Earrings

[1] Follow the pattern in figure 2 to make two panels. Do not end the tails.
[2] Refer to figure 5, a–b to make the fringe, using the 16-in. (41cm) tail at the bottom of a panel. Secure the tail in the beadwork, and trim.

[3] To make a loop at the top, thread a needle on the remaining tail, and stitch through the beadwork to exit between the two middle beads (c–d). Pick up four color B cylinders, sew back into the beadwork in the same place, and sew through two more beads (d–e). Retrace the thread path, then secure the thread, and trim.
[4] Open the loop of an earring finding (Basics), attach the earring, and close the loop.
[5] Repeat steps 2–4 to make a second earring to match the first.

EDITOR'S NOTE:
If you stitch the panels on a loom, you may be able to stitch more than one strap panel on a single set of warps, depending on the size of your loom. Stitch the first panel near the top of the loom, and end the working thread, leaving a 16-in. (41cm) tail. Drop down 8–12 in. (20–30cm), secure a new thread, and stitch another panel. Repeat, if you have space. When you cut the work off the loom, be sure to leave the tails on each end of the panel long enough that you can weave them in.

Contributors

Gail Ainsworth/Krutka is from Wendell, Mass. Contact her in care of Kalmbach Books.

Contact Amy Austin in care of Kalmbach Books.

Sharon Bateman is from Rathdrum, Idaho. Contact her via e-mail at sharonbateman.com.

Mary Bedford has been making jewelry for more than 20 years. One of her favorite techniques is using seed beads to blend colors together. Contact her via e-mail at mary.alice.bedford@gmail.com.

Maggie Beese contributes her work to local groups for fundraisers. Contact her via e-mail at maggiebeese@yahoo.com.

Paulette Biedenbender has been beading since 1997, and has been published in various beading publications. She continues to design jewelry and also teaches throughout the Milwaukee metro area. Contact her at h8winters@sbcglobal.net or visit her website, beadtrotters.com.

Bobbi Bongard is a graphic designer, sculptor, and avid jewelry artist living in midtown Manhattan. Contact her via e-mail at bobbibongard@gmail.com.

Lisa Brideau is from Middleton, Wis. Contact her in care of Kalmbach Books.

A great fan of all things plaid, Dorion Cable may or may not actually be Scottish. Her projects may be found at shefightslikeagirl.com.

Contact Antonio A. Calles in care of Kalmbach Books.

Giuseppe Chemello is from Torre Balfredo, Italy, and likes to share his beading patterns. Visit his website, spaghetticlay.com.

Pamela Cottrell is from Clinton, Ind. Contact her in care of Kalmbach Books.

Donna Coverdale is from Parkton, N.C. Contact her via e-mail at ladymadona@aol.com.

Jennifer Creasey began beading in 1991 and especially enjoys designing patterns with Alaskan and Native American themes. When she's not beading, she crochets or cross stitches. Visit Jennifer's website, polarbeads.com.

Contact Isabee T. Demski in care of Kalmbach Books.

Danielle Easley is from Albuquerque, N.M. Contact her in care of Kalmbach Books.

Rev. Wendy Ellsworth is a full-time studio seed bead artist living in Bucks County, Pa. Visit her website at ellsworthstudios.com.

Pennie Espiritu has been crafting and beading most of her life, and learned her skills from her grandmother. She teaches at a local college and works for Jo-Ann Fabrics. Visit her websites, lespirit-design.com and artfire.com/LeSpirit.

David Farnsworth is from Rochester, N.Y. Contact him in care of Kalmbach Books.

Amy Farnum has been beading since 1990. She specializes in loomwork and bead embroidery with size 15° beads. Contact her at amy@amfarnumdesigns.com or visit her website, amfarnumdesigns.com.

Lois A. Fetters is a beading addict who can be contacted via e-mail at geanfet@mail.riverview.net.

Ronit Florence is a Canadian-based beadwork artist who specializes in off-loom beading techniques and designing peyote stitch patterns. Contact Ronit via e-mail at ronit_florence@yahoo.ca.

Shannon T. Francis is from Tahlequa, Okla. Contact her in care of Kalmbach Books.

Ellen Friedenberg a proud contributor to Bead&Button. She lives in New York City and can be reached at ellenbeads@gmail.com.

Contact Gina Gavin in care of Kalmbach Books.

Julie Glasser is a beadweaving artist who has been teaching off-loom stitching since 2002. Visit her website, julieglasser.com.

Carol Green learned loomwork when she started her second career at Meant to Bead in Toledo, Ohio, in 2004. She retired again at age 80, but still enjoys beading. Contact her via e-mail at cgreen4@juno.com.

Robin Griffes likes to spend her time making seed bead jewelry. Contact her via e-mail at robin2004griffes62@yahoo.com, or visit robin.artfire.com.

Rita Grossberg is a full-time beader and fine artist who uses her watercolor paintings as inspiration for pattern designs. Contact her via e-mail at reg486@comcast.net.

Pascale Guichaoua-Mikovic is from La Mulatière, France. Contact her via e-mail at perlicoti.canalblog.com.

Rhonda Guy is a mixed-media artist known for her beadwork, polymer clay, and miniatures. Her work is sold at Damselfly Gallery, Midway, Ky. Contact her via e-mail at beadbug@windstream.net.